# MILLENNIALS ON BOARD:

**The Impact Of The Rising Generation On The Workplace.**

**Rachel I. Reiser**

Published by Intern Bridge, Inc.

## Millennials on Board:
## The Impact Of The Rising Generation On The Workplace

By Rachel I. Reiser

ISBN 978-0-9799373-4-7

First Printing January 2010

Published by Intern Bridge, Inc.
19 Railroad Street, Suite 3B
Acton, MA 01720

For sales information, please email Sales@InternBridge.com or call us at 800-531-6091.

Cover design/layout/production:
web.me.com/bookpackgraphics/Bookpack_Graphics

Printed in U.S.A.

In loving memory of my sister, Ilyana,
whose writer's voice I always hear.

# ACKNOWLEDGEMENTS

There are many people to whom I am grateful for their support for this project. I must start with the many Starbucks in the Boston area where I spent more than my share of weekend days – laptop and tote bag of books in hand – working on this book. It seems that for me, like for many writers, a "skinny vanilla latte" and a different environment is conducive to my productivity.

Of course, my thanks go out to all of those managers and Millennials who were willingly interviewed, sharing thoughts and ideas based on your experiences in your respective workplaces. Your insights were considerable and gave me much food for thought; you are quoted herein, and I know that you will provide lots of considerations for readers. I also thank my students; you excitedly gave your permissions to quote your reactions to the experiment of living technology-free, even if just for a day.

I am indebted to my colleagues over the years, who have always been sources of stimulation and motivation in our professional work ... and lots of fun, too. I am particularly thankful to my supervisors, past and present, who have been nothing less than encouraging as I have pursued my interest and work in this area, and to Babson College, a place that is tremendously supportive of professional growth and development. I'd also like to thank my early readers, who gave me very useful feedback and opinions that helped this project to gel, and to my publisher, Rich Bottner, who got this train rolling by approaching me to do this.

Finally, I'd like to thank my very loving friends and family. You have always inspired me and supported me, including enthusiastically engaging in about a million conversations on Millennials, even when it seemed that I might be able to talk of nothing else. Your encouragement helped to make this happen, and for this and so much else, I love you all very much!

# TABLE OF CONTENTS

# FOREWORD

**by Helen Drinan, President of Simmons College and Former President of the Society for Human Resources Management**

With more than thirty years of strategic human resource management behind me, I am now the President of Simmons College in Boston, Massachusetts. This combined experience informs my perspective on the world of work for which we are preparing our students, many of whom are now Millennials. So when I was asked to provide a foreword for this important book, I thought perhaps weaving together observations on both academia and human resources might position this valuable information in its most useful context.

More than half the time I spent in human resources involved increasing leadership responsibility in banking during the period of consolidation that has changed the face of U.S. financial services. I learned critical lessons about the workforce that have now been translated into most of the 90% of the national economy which is service based. Far from the days when people were an incidental factor of the productive input of our economy, people are now the critical element of organizational success. The talent of our workforce is the only aspect of competitive advantage not quickly reproducible by others. Simply stated, talent is the difference between success and failure for the vast majority of for-profit and not-for-profit organizations in the United States today.

Given the compelling nature of this truth, it has been the case for some time that the pursuit and retention of best talent is the top cited CEO (Chief Executive Officer) issue, both in the United States and in most other developed nations. A literal "war for talent" has been waged among the most competitive employers, and the demand for and shortage of skilled workers has been seen as a determinant of both organizational and national success. While it is true that times of economic challenge take some of the pressure off competitive labor forces, it is also true that the smartest employers know how to capitalize on economic hardship, and move to "guerilla warfare," if you will—that is, the continuous evaluation and replacement of current employees, seeking to opportunistically upgrade even as the size of the overall workforce is being reduced. Seen in this light, the war for talent is very much a survival process, suggesting that those employers who win the best talent are most likely to survive on the increasingly competitive world stage. High stakes undertaking, this talent competition.

If the global picture shows us a continuous demand for talent, how are we as a nation preparing our citizens to participate? The answer for us right now is fortunate—with the best higher education system the world has ever seen. However, just as with the auto industry of fifty years ago, we cannot rest on our laurels here—competition for our number one position has grown enormously, with fewer foreign students studying here, and many more foreign universities setting up competitive programs to keep their own talent local. Aware of this, we in higher education have been working hard to establish performance and accountability measures which advance the success of our students and hold our feet to the fire in making the contributions necessary for national competitiveness. We have much work to do, but we have at least heard the message. We have reason to be optimistic.

Having a clear relationship between organizations which seek talent, and a higher education system which produces it, does not tell the whole story. In fact, corporations spend more money on training and development than is spent in the higher education system nationally, principally because the work conducted in higher education is not sufficiently robust to meet the detailed demands of the work of such organizations. Think of it this way: even after graduation from master's level preparation, most new employees will need months of time to acquire organizationally specific knowledge that is necessary to be competent. From this fact, though, we learn something critical from best-practice development organizations. To move beyond competence to top performance, the learning opportunities have to be organizationally and individually relevant. In other words, same size fits all development ends in the classroom, while customization of learning is the only economically feasible choice in the process of top talent development. Why? Because organizations have learned that the classroom experience is not the primary way people learn in a real work environment. All the so-called book learning gets put to the test in the real world, and once that test has been given, only then can personalized development needs be identified. Further, we have known for a long time that learning styles differ from individual to individual, so while we can generalize some methodologies, they must be applied individually.

With highly customized development initiatives, best practice organizations have recognized that part of the solution to effective individualized training relates to demographic variables. While it is ultimately necessary that organizations present a uniform face to customers, they have learned that preparing Millennials for this takes different development interventions than those required to prepare Boomers for the very same experience. Given how high the stakes are in attracting and retaining key talent, this kind of customization is a base line requirement for best practice organizations. In fact, it offers an opportunity to attract seemingly disparate talent styles while working toward an outcome that capitalizes on the strengths of each. So, rather than seeking cookie-cutter sameness in their talent searches, they can expand their talent pools to all demographics, drawing on the broadest definition of top talent. This is perhaps yet a new way of thinking about inclusiveness and its contribution to best outcomes.

The personality embodied by the Millennials calls for the workplace to take a new look at how we work with our new employees. We need to understand the Millennials' approach to the world - in particular, what they expect of their professional opportunities and environments. To understand who they are is an essential ingredient in working effectively with them. In our efforts to best cultivate and exploit the talents of Millennial employees, we need to manage their expectations and help them deal with stress and disappointment, all while capitalizing on their determination and talents. Millennials' recent arrival in the work milieu brings with it a climate change that cannot be denied and suggests response and adaptation from the "way things have always been done." This presents much opportunity to develop and grow as organizations.

I believe that we in higher education are in a position to advance work on demographic development planning, and can make a significant contribution earlier in the learning process before employers take over. As higher education continues to self evaluate and transform, this is a key opportunity to align more directly with important workforce development strategies that afford competitive advantage to us as a nation.

# INTRODUCTION

## Millennials - The Intriguing Generation?

**W**e've heard them called Generation Y, Generation NeXt, Echo Boomers, Boomlets, and Millennials, among other nomenclature, but I can never forget the first time I heard about them as a group. It was November of 2001, and I was in Chicago at a professional conference about undergraduate business curriculum, a topic that I did not find particularly enthralling, but that I attended as a function of my job at the time. One of the available breakout sessions, entitled "Understanding & Responding to the New Millennials," was offered by colleagues from Virginia Tech. In this session, the presenters discussed the work of Neil Howe and William Strauss, well known experts on the field of generational studies. My passion was born that day!

This session introduced me, in a salient and cohesive way, to research that explained this generation of students' unique and influential psychographic dynamics. My professional life has been spent in many facets of higher education administration, educating students and supervising employees of all ages. During this time I have worked directly with college students and really experienced firsthand the changing characteristics of today's late adolescent. But never, until this session in Chicago, had I been presented with information that so immediately resonated with what I was experiencing with my students. I now had concrete language that described the growing trends towards ultra-achievement, hyper-scheduling, excessive parental involvement and attachment, high expectations for themselves and others, team-approach, optimism, and a disproportionate orientation toward technology.

Once back at home in Boston, I immediately purchased Strauss and Howe's recent publication, *Millennials Rising: The Next Great Generation*, and began my research. In the years since then, I have found hundreds of books, articles, and news programs that have focused attention on this fascinating population. I do not seem to be alone in my curiosity about Millennials and what makes them tick, which isn't very surprising; we, as a society, have been captivated by this generation since their initial year of birth in 1982 when, according to Strauss and Howe, they were already being touted as the "Great Class of 2000"[1] in reference to their long-impending high school graduation. No prior generation had been identified from their very beginning, but Millennials have been different from the start. And our attention on them has been different, too.

So, some of the basics: their birth years are generally defined as 1982 to 2002; they are a large population and, with immigration, will likely end up being one-third larger than the Baby Boomer Generation; also as a result of immigration, along with other factors, they are racially and ethnically more diverse than any previous generation; the initial Millennials were raised by Boomer parents, while the latter Millennials will be raised by Generation X-ers.

For the past 11 years, Beloit College in Wisconsin has put out what they call the "Mindset List," an effort to identify the worldview of 18-year-olds entering college that year. This always makes the rounds via e-mail amongst college administrators and provides some interesting and fun food for thought. When I talk about Millennials, I often share some of these "factoids" – some from Beloit and some of my own – that I think really identify how Millennials are a whole new brand, generationally speaking.

- They have always known banking to be done via ATM's.

- They associate "viruses" with computers.

- There has always been a national holiday honoring Martin Luther King, Jr.

- Caller ID has always been available.

- Forget mix tapes; it's all about the Playlists!

---

[1] Neil Howe and William Strauss, *Millennials Rising: The Next Great Generation*, (New York: Vintage Books, 2000).

- They have always been able to get round-the-clock coverage of practically anything on cable.

- The Berlin Wall?

- McDonald's never came in Styrofoam containers.

- There has always been a pharmaceutical treatment for AIDS.

- There have always been red M&Ms, and blue ones are not new. And there used to be beige ones?

- They have always cooked their popcorn in a microwave.

- Searching for the right job takes place online.

These bits of information tell a lot. As managers of this new generation, it is incumbent upon us to understand Millennials in order to most effectively supervise them. These outlooks and experiences are a part of what makes them who they are, along with the basic demographics, but there is of course so much more to discuss regarding what gives them a generational culture.

*Millennials on Board* examines just who Millennials are in the deeper sense by looking at this unique generation in a new way, considering prevalent research, and discerning how societal influences and educational systems are contributing to the generational characteristics and their implications for the workplace. I am fascinated by the societal factors that have, in my opinion, helped to form the psychography of the generation, and by discussing and analyzing the myriad of information that has been published and promoted about the generation, I provide a context for companies and managers. In preparing for this project, I read hundreds of books and articles, interviewed dozens of managers and human resources representatives from various industries, and talked with early Millennials who are currently in the workplace.

All of this information, coupled with my own extensive experience working hands-on with these young people as an educator and as a supervisor, provides me with tangible ideas and suggestions for ways that companies can understand their Millennial employees, in order to work with them and integrate them into the overall organizational culture. In contrast, and perhaps even more importantly, there are ways in which companies can work within their own organization, integrating it into the overall Millennial culture. As I often say, "this train is moving, and we need to get on board!"

Many of the books and articles that I reviewed appeal to me as an educator and a counselor for students on the cusp of adulthood, in addition to my role as a supervisor of Millennials and non-Millennials. There is a huge audience for academic works about the Millennial generation, and I cannot seem to walk into a bookstore and leave without at least one or two new volumes for my library. Yet there is not a lot of material out there that takes all of this data, discusses it in layman's terms, and considers the implications for the workplace environment. Business organizations thirst for an understanding of who these young employees are, what makes them tick, and how to incorporate them into the existing organizational culture. How do we maintain a healthy and productive multi-generational workplace when this new generation is so different from all those who have come before? And how will the workplace evolve as Millennials are more and more prevalent in the organization, even leading the company in some cases (and will be more and more over the coming years)? These are the questions with which we are now faced.

I understand that many may feel that there is a lot of generalization involved in these discussions. In fact, when I have spoken with audiences including young Millennials, some react to feeling stereotyped...but most validate the findings with gusto. It's important to recognize, as with any kind of research, that there are indeed generalities and questions that arise from the data, both quantitative and qualitative. At the root of generational research is the concept that, within a generation, people develop a "peer personality," in which they share events during their formative years, (usually between 10 to 18 years old), that in turn have an impact on their value system and psychographic profile as a group. Even this very notion raises questions for some.

> *"Here's what I don't get....Defining a generation seems rather arbitrary. I can accept that there is some age range of peers with whom I have commonality. But the starting year is arbitrary. For example, if the Millennial generation is 1982 to 2002, I presume there is a differently named generation from 1962 to 1982. And then wouldn't there be just as valid a segment from 1972 to 1992 and 1992 to 2012? And isn't someone at the bottom end of a span more likely to have more in common with someone at the top end of the next span down than someone at the top of their own span? I've wrestled with this definition of generations in my mind for some time."*
>
> Frank Vitiello
> President, Vitech, Inc.

I might argue that there are truths to this critique. Depending upon the researchers, generational time spans can be defined with different years, but are generally only a few years off from each other. And there is, of course, overlap in generationally-ascribed characteristics for someone "on the cusp" of two different generations. Finally, just as in many topics of research, there are generalizations – I would never claim that the psychography is "one size fits all." Anyone who works with generational studies struggles with these questions to some extent. But, as with any academic research, there are some basic principles that are universally accepted – questions and all. We need to remember that the notion of generational culture is widely accepted and the temporal spans are driven by the generational definitions that have evolved over time, with more recent historic attention being paid to Boomers, followed by Gen X, and then Millennials *– the three generations that currently pervade the multi-generational workplace.* There are generations that preceded Boomers, of course, but I believe that it is with the Boomer generation that attention started being paid to these notions at a higher level, and the more significant academic, cultural, and organizational conversations began.

One can't talk about the challenges of understanding Millennials without discussing another essential criticism. As I have read about and researched the Millennial Generation, I have been struck by the fact that the qualities, both good and bad, that are most consistently ascribed to them may be most relevant to those in the middle class through the affluent in our society. In fact, my biggest critique of Strauss and Howe's research is that it focused on way too narrow a sample. When I talk with audiences from all different industries – education, corporate, government, human resources – we frequently come to similar conclusions: many of the traits that are analyzed in the research on Millennials do not necessarily include the issues endemic to those struggling financially in our society. The pressures of success at all costs, managing frenzied activity schedules, and "keeping up with the Joneses" are not necessarily the issues of those who live on the economic margins of our society. The stresses that come with not getting an "A" on every single paper or hustling from soccer practice to a violin lesson to a tutoring session may not be of paramount concern to a young person from a family struggling to keep a roof over their heads. There are many people being left out of the conversation as we discuss Millennials. As Annette Lareau discusses in her book, *Unequal Childhoods*, "[f]ormidable economic constraints make it a major life task for (working class) parents to put food on the table, arrange for housing, negotiate unsafe neighborhoods, take children to the doctor (often waiting for city buses that do not come), clean children's clothes, and get children to bed and have them ready for school the next morning. But unlike middle-class parents, these adults do not consider the concerted development of children, particularly through organized leisure activities, an essential aspect of good parenting."[2]

These disparities are of significant concern to me, and certainly socioeconomic difference plays a very large role in addressing psychographic distinctions within an overall generation. Nonetheless, I have found that the themes I discuss when I present to groups or consult with organizations resonate quite deeply, just as they had for me when I first heard of Millennials in November of 2001, and there are some trends that have begun to cross socio-economic lines. The issues that are raised have relevance...to parents, educators, and certainly to employers! Thus, I focus a lot of attention in this book on the themes that we see among the more prototypical Millennials.

It is challenging to ponder these issues amidst such uncertain economic times. It is clear to everyone, regardless of our background in economic theory, that we are experiencing a period in our economic history that is new to most of us, and certainly a new phenomenon for Millennials. But what does it mean for them? Will it change their psychography or outlook

---

[2] Annette Lareau, *Unequal Childhoods: Class, Race, and Family Life,*
(California: University of California Press, 2003).

on various issues? Will they become less optimistic? Will they become less dependent on parental support – monetarily and emotionally – since they may have to rally their own internal resources? Having fewer professional options and opportunity, and the resulting decrease in expendable income, will they become less socially responsible in their consumer and professional decisions? Obviously, it is early to start raising these questions, and there really isn't much data out there about it yet. I have my own ideas, which, of course, I share at relevant points in the chapters that follow, but this is certainly another way that the current economic situation suggests the need for further research into this uncharted territory.

One last, and essential, caveat to protect me from the readers who may be a Millennial or a parent of a Millennial (or even a "Helicopter Parent"... we'll get to that!): remember, we could have a critical discussion of any generation, talking about the highlights and hurdles of the characteristics of its members. In fact, Generation X – the generation that precedes Millennials and happens to include me – does not fare very well in the research or in the public perception. Being characterized as an angry, jaded slacker does not do a whole lot for my sense of self. Fortunately, I am not writing about Gen X-ers, so my ego can stay intact! This book is about Millennials, and as such I will find comfort in dissecting their cumulative personality and psychography, and discussing its implications for your workplaces. All of us Gen X-ers, Boomers, etc. can rest easy for another day, at least until the Millennials take over – as they will – and tell us all that is wrong with us! We'll see if they find us as intriguing as we find them.

# CHAPTER ONE

## Millennials - The Hovered Generation?

**A** few years ago a colleague of mine, Carol, was meeting with a student – we'll call her Stephanie – to discuss her course selection for the coming semester. As they reviewed some of the options, it was clear that one of the decisions Stephanie needed to make was to choose from two different sections of a course that she needed to take. Let me be clear here...Stephanie was choosing between two different sections of the same class, taught by the same professor, one offered at 9:15 AM on Tuesdays and Thursdays, and the other offered on the same days of the week at 11:30 AM. Let me be really clear here...the **only** difference between the two classes was that one ran about two hours before the other. Stephanie was not sure what to do and told Carol that she needed to call her mom. Carol suggested, as I think any reasonable person would suggest in such a situation, that Stephanie make a choice at that time and come back later and try to make alterations if she changed her mind. So Stephanie chose a section, they got her registered, and she went on her merry way. One might think it ends here, but the story continues. The next day, Stephanie returned and met with Carol again. She had spoken with her mom, and her mom felt that the other section was more appropriate/better/more preferable...whatever. Stephanie asked to change her registration to the other section.

In the end, I don't really care what the reasoning was for making the change; that isn't really what is important here. What is important, and is, in fact, a bit worrisome, is that Stephanie was paralyzed in making this relatively minor decision. And Stephanie is not alone; I could go on and on with hundreds of stories from my experiences and those of my colleagues around the nation that illustrate this same point: Millennials are sheltered. They have wonderfully close relationships with their families, and feel truly supported, but they have little experience figuring things out for themselves. And they and their families often perpetuate this arrested development long after they reach young adulthood. We may assume that this is behavior that a young person would grow out of as they leave high school and get adjusted to college, but in fact what we see is that college students are more than willing to cede control or decision-making to their parents (at least around the majority of issues) – and that it doesn't stop at commencement in May four years later.

These very involved parents are known, originally among college administrators but now in mainstream media, as "Helicopter Parents" because they seem to be constantly hovering. This term, originally attributed to Wake Forest Dean Mary Gerady, has been expanded to include "Blackhawk Parents," the ones who hover overhead but occasionally zip down to strike, and "Submarine Parents," who lurk hidden underneath the surface but rise up from time to time to torpedo. There is a lot of discussion about these so-called Helicopter Parents, by college administrators and faculty, employers, and parents themselves. I think all agree, at least when really thinking it through rather than reacting viscerally to a particularly unpleasant encounter, that these parents are generally working with what they believe to be their child's best interest at heart and, by being so explicitly involved in their child's life, they are doing precisely what they have always been told is their role and responsibility as a parent. Think of the messaging that they receive.

The September 2007 issue of *Boston Magazine* published the featured article about the "Best Schools" in the Boston area, grabbing the attention of parents with a cover shot of a smiling pre-school age child with these bold words emblazoned above her head: "Gotta Start 'Em Young; Why It's Never Too Early to Stress About Your Child's Education." Below that, in smaller print, were the words "The Hub's Top Preschools." Preschools!

How can parents not get caught up in the hysteria with messaging like this? And it doesn't stop with preschool. Parents of children of all ages are barraged with messages – increasingly over the past couple of decades – that they need to be continually involved in all of the aspects of their children's lives, and to always be a strong advocate for their children. I hear from parents all the time that the school attended by their children has an overtly stated expectation of parental involvement with classroom activities, with the Parent-Teacher Organization, and with their individual child's academic life. This is all very appropriate, in my estimate, and is a role that parents should take, especially with their younger children. So how does it happen that we now have this notion of "Helicopter Parents?" Aren't they doing what they are told, by their kids' teachers, principals, and society at large? Are some going overboard? Have they been told that there is no such thing as bad involvement or too much involvement? Have the parents been so conditioned to advocacy that they find it difficult to hang back and let go as their children get older and need to take on more responsibility themselves? The recent embrace of the very language of "Helicopter Parent," with all of its pejorative implication, underscores our own conflict around this issue. On one hand, parents are told in so many ways that this is what it means to be a parent, and then, at the very next turn, they are criticized for their over-involvement and labeled a Helicopter Parent.

But the fact is, despite all of this reasonable debate, that many parents' level of involvement in the lives of their adult children is often perceived as too much – not just bothersome to those of us working with the adult child in question, but sometimes even concerning. I am not alone in my surprise with the increasing role of parents in their college-age children's education over the course of the last decade or so of my career. But again, I must remind myself of what society has suggested represents "good parenting," and just how strong that messaging has been. I and my colleagues in various institutions of higher education often remind ourselves of the unique challenge new college students face in their very quick transition to semi-adulthood: they graduate from high school one day in May as a kid, and somehow, over the course of a few short summer months, they are expected to become adults (albeit young ones), faced with new self-sufficiency and responsibility as they begin their college career in September. We are quite appreciative and understanding of what an undertaking this is, and thus are tolerant and promoting of the growth required for the huge developmental transition. What we are less understanding of is the transition for their parents. Here these parents have been major players in the life and education of their "kid" for all of these years, constantly receiving the message that good parenting equals involved parenting, and now they are expected to make this very abrupt philosophical change. And yet we don't understand why it is tough for them. (Never mind that in most cases they are also footing a pretty hefty bill for the child's education, so of course have a vested financial interest in addition to their personal one.)

One tremendous outcome of all of this is the apparent closeness between many Millennials and their families, especially with their parents.

Technology has enabled a lot of the deep and ongoing connection. According to a 2006 article for *Newsweek* magazine by Barbara Kantrowitz and Peg Tyre, a survey of Middlebury College first-year students reported an average of over ten communications per week with their parents, "over cell phone, e-mail, Instant Messenger, dorm phone, text messaging and postal mail. Parents initiate most of this contact, Hofer found, but their children don't seem to mind; most students said they were satisfied with the amount of communication they had with their parents and 28 percent wanted even more with their fathers."[3] When I was in college, I spoke to my parents maybe once a week – on Sundays, when the rates were cheaper. If I had some issue or problem at some point during that week, by the time that Sunday phone call rolled around I usually worked it out myself and it was either long forgotten, or I was able to provide the "all's well that ends well" recap. But this is not the case now, and with so many tech mediums available for communication the continued closeness is much more easily facilitated. College students engage their parents in their daily lives in ways that hadn't been possible previously, and it has implications for their personal problem solving. For example, 38 percent of 400 students polled online acknowledged that their parents had either called into, or physically attended, meetings with academic advisors.[4] Remember, these are college students; this raises the question of appropriateness. Is it too much? As someone who has been involved in college student academic advising for many years, I might suggest that 38 percent of the advising meetings that I have been a part of were not centered around issues of such significance that parental involvement was required. This all comes from a good place and from what I think is great progress for family life in the United States; after all, children in coupled families are receiving more combined attention from their parents today than children did 25 years ago – 6 hours per workday in 2002 versus 5 hours in 1977.[5] I am quite admiring of these close relationships, but they may have some costs, as well.

---

[3] Barbara Kantrowitz and Peg Tyre, "The Fine Art of Letting Go," *Newsweek*, May 22, 2006.

[4] Experience Inc., "Helicopter Poll," January 2006.

[5] Families and Work Institute, *Generation and Gender in the Workplace*, (Families and Work Institute and The American Business Collaboration, 2004).

*"This past summer I offered an internship to an engineering student that was over 400 miles away from where her family lived. She was provided the offer of a lifetime ... [g]reat pay, benefits, downtown corporate condo, chance to work with several other college students and a chance to work under the supervision of some of the top senior engineers in the company. Despite being a rising senior (one year from finishing school), and despite having left home to attend college in a neighboring state, she was urged strongly by her parents to turn down the position. They felt it was too far for her to live on her own outside the bubble of a "college" or "university" atmosphere. Was it a big step? Absolutely. What to do – what to do??? The student, admittedly nervous herself, truly wanted the position. She knew just how big an opportunity it was and so did we. We also knew that with the 'helicopter parents' of the Millennial today, we had to do something to encourage them to accept this as a good thing as much as we had to encourage the student to overcome the nerves. We began by setting up phone calls with the managers the student would be working under. We answered questions, asked some ourselves, and built a great relationship with them to start out. Between myself and my boss, the managers the student worked for, and the family themselves, we ended up establishing what they felt was a great support network for her if she decided to come. We also set up a conference call with a student about the same age who worked in a similar situation a year earlier. We provided information regarding the number of students who she would be around on a day in day out basis, information about the city and specifics about the living accommodations themselves. What I feel was the icing on the cake was when we turned to technology. We had a camera installed on the laptop she was given for the assignment and had one of our local IT folks do the same for the family's home PC. Since they were loaners we had available, we did not incur any additional cost aside from the gas it cost to drive to their home and the time it took to install. Establishing the comfort level with the family was ultimately what made the student say yes."*

Bill Phillips, Sr. Recruiting Specialist
(Strategic Talent Development)
Duke Energy Corporation

The kind of parents that I am discussing endeavor to remain pretty involved throughout the college experience – and, fair or not, get labeled as "Helicopter Parents" in the process. Subsequently, many have trouble making the break as their children leave college and hit the work world. So now business organizations are finding themselves surprised by the front-and-center role that the parents of their young employees take.

*"We have had employees show up with their parents, not for the interview but they bring them to it. I had one [whose] father drove her to the second interview and got them lost and so she was late. The father came in to take the blame and let me know it was his fault. We have made offers lately to new graduates who tell us they need to consult their parents or that their parents want them to ask certain questions – that type of thing. We are not planning to make any exceptions for this type of behavior; we feel it is inappropriate to have parents in the workplace unless invited after the fact by the employee; we are fine with visitors."*
Anonymous
HR Business Partner, Multimedia Publishing Company

Not all employers have the same experience, and I have certainly interviewed many who feel that the media attention on "Helicopter Parents" is exaggerated, but I have spoken with so many longtime professionals who have seen such a substantial increase in parental involvement that it is clear this is a topic worth contemplating. In fact, I would argue that parents are one of the two most influential forces in the psychography of the Millennial Generation. Of course, this is not surprising; parents have always had the ultimate influence in the shaping of their children – even in the collective societal shaping of a generation. The other most significant influence in my opinion is technology, and I will address that in a later chapter. But back to parents and their potential hefty sway.

We are remiss if we do not acknowledge socioeconomics in discussing parental involvement. It is evident from all the research that parents who are dealing with keeping the family's "head above water," financially-speaking, often do not have the time for the level of intrusion that I discuss here. There are larger family priorities – such as meeting the bills, putting food on the table and generally making ends meet – that inhibit this investment of time and energy. If a parent has to work overtime, or even two jobs, to ensure their family's survival, there just isn't the psychological space to devote to relentless involvement in the lives of their children, even if they wanted to. And this isn't necessarily a bad thing; in fact, as Medline Levine points out in her work *The Price of Privilege*, "the kind of anxious, overprotective, over-solicitous, intrusive parenting that has become commonplace in affluent communities actually diminishes a child's sense of efficacy and autonomy. Anxiety and its frequent companions, over-involvement and intrusion, combine to make a particularly lethal combination. This parenting style makes children hesitant to actively approach a world that the parent portrays as dangerous, and, as a consequence, it limits children's natural eagerness to try out new and challenging experiences."[6]

We must also recognize that these societal trends toward parental ultra-involvement are strong, and are even crossing over socioeconomic lines in a variety of ways. One interesting example of this ubiquitous influence: The *Boston Globe* recently reported on The Bottom Line, a Boston-based agency that employs recent college graduates as counselors for teenagers and young adults with the goal of providing them with the care and hand-holding that may make the difference in seeing them through to a college degree. "Since 19-year-old Roberto Green started his first semester of college in September, the calls and e-mails have come almost weekly. Just checking in to see how he's doing, how classes are going, whether he's running into any roadblocks. One week, he received a care package filled with candy bars, Pop-Tarts, and other treats. Another time, there was a face-to-face visit, and questions about grades, tuition payments, and spending habits. This attention has not come from one of those 'helicopter' parents, who hover over their college-aged children much like they did when their offspring were in kindergarten, but from a 20-something counselor who graduated from college not long ago herself."[7] Interestingly, this article sparked a lively online debate with readers, with some expressing approval of the development of programs like these that may help to bridge the gap somewhat between the "have's" and "have not's," others stating concern that this doesn't get to the root of issues of socioeconomic disparity and

---

[6]  Madeline Levine, Ph.D., *The Price of Privilege: How Parental Pressure and Material Advantage Are Creating a Generation of Disconnected and Unhappy Kids* (New York: HarperCollins Publishers, 2006).

[7]  James Vaznis, "College Counselors Fill the Role of Parent," *The Boston Globe*, December 8, 2008).

suggesting that the money be put into programs that teach parents how to be stronger resources for their children, and yet more who felt that this is just another phase of what they see as detrimental "helicopter parenting" - this time it just isn't the parents who are hovering. As one commenter explained: "I was a college student in the 1970's, and the current crop of helicopter parents is a symptom of what is wrong with education. Back then, parents and society figured an 18-year-old was equipped with the necessary skills to survive on a college campus (I was at UMass Amherst). I never would have dreamed of asking or allowing my parents to become involved with my issues, whether it was a roommate problem or a grade issue. I was a grown up. Sure, there were places and people I could go to for advice, my parents included, but the current educational philosophy keeps kids unaccountable and pampered for way too long. I[t] is fine to give the[m] 'roots and wings,' but not at the cost of making them unnecessarily dependent. ... Let's start making kids responsible and independent EARLIER, not after we send them away to college, unequipped to make decisions and act as young adults. Sure, advisors and parents should be available, but it seems the student should know when to ask for help. This constant checking would have seemed insulting to my generation."[8]

This reader taps into what has been discussed ad nauseam among parents, educators, and employers...what might we be doing to our kids with all of this parental over-involvement and intrusion? As discussed in Dr. Levine's findings, apparently a lot that may not be so good.

*"I would have to say that as a contingent worker service provider, we see this a lot. We are almost in locus parenti. Not only do they look to their employment manager, but they trust almost immediately. What I think happens is that they really get sheltered so much, that they do not realize that it's not about them, it's about business. For example, if a position dissolves, sometimes this is due to performance, but sometimes it is based on business need. This has been especially true during the economic slump and it hits this group the hardest."*
Cynthia Levinson
On-Site Supervisor at State Street Corporation, Kelly Complete

---

[8] Reader comment to "College Counselors Fill the Role of Parent," *The Boston Globe*, December 8, 2008 [http://people.boston.com/articles/cityandregion/?p=articlecomments&activityId=8600750770905467552].

Perhaps most importantly, Millennials struggle with disappointment, as they have in many cases been sheltered from such experiences throughout their formative years. With such protection, they haven't had much occasion to experience letdowns, and their coping skills are somewhat deficient as a result.

*"In years past, not hearing feedback from a manager meant that you were 'taking care of business.' Now it leaves younger employees feeling 'disconnected' or 'insecure' about how they are doing. Constant feedback to the Millennial Generation equals reassurance! Even if the feedback isn't always great, the feedback and the fact that someone takes the time out to give them the feedback on a regular basis make them feel like they matter. So what have we done to conform to the preferences of the 'future' of our company? We are currently implementing Mentorship Programs within all of our lines of business. Assigning someone a mentor when they come in we feel is critical to the Millennials' success and critical to our success as a company. They are a source of constant support and feedback and a resource to use as the new employee acclimates his or herself into their new career. We have also implemented new hire rotational programs. The teams who manage these programs play a more involved role with the new hires similar to the way our Intern/Co-op program and its students were handled. While these positions are full-time permanent roles, they are a four-term rotational role that gives the students exposure to different areas within their field of expertise. They are evaluated more closely to determine where their strengths and weaknesses are and trained in those areas to become better assets to our company. It truly is a win-win situation for us and them!"*
Bill Phillips, Sr. Recruiting Specialist
(Strategic Talent Development)
Duke Energy Corporation

Hara Estroff Marano writes in *A Nation of Wimps,* "parents are anxious and hyperattentive to their kids, reacting to every little blip of their child's day, eager to solve every problem for their child – and believe that's good parenting."[9] She goes on to quote David Anderegg, a psychology profes-

---

[9]  Hara Estroff Marano, *A Nation of Wimps: The High Cost of Invasive Parenting* (New York: Broadway Books, 2008).

sor and child psychologist, who authored the book *Worried All the Time*: "'If you have an infant and the baby has gas, burping the baby is being a good parent. But when you have a ten-year-old who has metaphorical gas, you don't burp them. You have to let them sit with it, try to figure out what to do about it. They then learn to tolerate moderate amounts of difficulty, and it's not the end of the world.'"[10] I fully understand the challenge for parents in sitting and seemingly just watching their child try to work their way through a difficult issue – it is not easy to hold back from stepping in and helping to resolve the problem, but it has been evidenced that this is not of long-term benefit to the child. Unfortunately, we have seen that this metaphorical burping doesn't cease as that ten-year-old grows to young adulthood, and that has significant consequences for their long-term development and maturity. Madeline Levine, Ph.D. writes in *The Price of Privilege* that "[o]verinvolvement is not simply 'more' healthy involvement; rather it is involvement that can get in the way of child development. It is an umbrella term, often used to cover a wide range of overzealous parenting activities, ranging from the relatively benign to the downright disastrous."[11] She goes on to state, "[i]t is usually, but not always, ill advised, and some children can be remarkably forgiving of this sort of behavior."[12] I suggest that all too many children are way too forgiving of it; I find that the average college student of the last decade has not only forgiven parental overinvolvement, but has in fact encouraged it. Like Stephanie allowing her mother to decide which class time is better for her, many Millennials have quite willingly turned the reins of many aspects of their lives over to their parents, and I fear that now they don't want to – or don't know how to – reclaim them, though they have reached full adulthood.

There is an interesting, and rather titillating, article entitled "Scenes from the Culture Clash" that provides some extreme and entertaining examples of parental "overinvolvement" with their adult children in the workplace. I put overinvolvement in quotes because these stories are so excessive that no reasonable person would try to justify them. My favorite: "A 22-year-old pharmaceutical employee learned that he was not getting

[10] Ibid.

[11] Madeline Levine, Ph.D., *The Price of Privilege: How Parental Pressure and Material Advantage Are Creating a Generation of Disconnected and Unhappy Kids* (New York: HarperCollins Publishers, 2006).

[12] Ibid.

the promotion he had been eyeing. His boss told him he needed to work on his weaknesses first. The Harvard grad had excelled at everything he had ever done, so he was crushed by the news. He told his parents about the performance review, and they were convinced there was some misunderstanding, some way they could fix it, as they'd been able to fix everything before. His mother called the human-resources department the next day. Seventeen times. She left increasingly frustrated messages: 'You're purposely ignoring us'; 'you fudged the evaluation'; 'you have it in for my son.' She demanded a mediation session with her, her son, his boss, and HR – and got it. At one point, the 22-year-old reprimanded the HR rep for being 'rude to my mom.'"[13] This seems to be too much to me; I argue that the organization should have simply informed the employee's mother that they would work directly with their employee regarding any concerns that he might have, declined the meeting that she wished to have, and followed up directly with the employee himself, including stating that they do not work with the parents of employees on such matters. This could provide an excellent learning experience for the employee on professionalism and perhaps for his mother as well. And of course it bears mention that it is these ridiculous and unusual stories that enable the perpetuation of nomenclature like "Helicopter Parent;" it is sensationalist media that captures the attention of the general public – this is undeniable. But the thing is, while these stories may seem absurd and wacky, I hear from many employers of Millennials that they have experiences with similar interference from parents, albeit to a much lesser degree, and actually many have come to see it as the norm and have even embraced it to some degree.

> *"On numerous occasions I have had parents approach our career booth to drop off their child's resume and 'pitch' their qualifications. We were surprised when we first started seeing parents show up at career fairs three years ago. Most recently I was surprised when just this fall I had a parent approach me at a master's level career fair! The parent was dropping their child's resume off at each table during her lunch break and wanted to see if there would be a fit for her child with the organization. She was also talking to companies to better understand what they do and what they were looking for. I'm not sure how much it helps the candidate find a job but I do believe it helps the parent understand which companies might be a better match."* (cont. on page 28)

---

[13] Danielle Sacks, "Scenes from the Culture Clash," *Fast Company*, January 2006.

*(cont. from page 27)*

*"Parents have now become their child's 'agent' and they feel very tied to their child's success. I have heard of some instances where recruiters have looked down on this practice and will not even entertain a resume that comes through this venue (some refer to this practice as 'pimping your child's career'), but we actually embrace this phenomenon because we understand how important it is for a parent to feel comfortable. Of course this accommodation greatly depends on the situation – we understand if the student is attending school in another state, but if the student just couldn't roll out of bed, that's another matter all together."*

Helen Hong
College Relations Manager, WellPoint Inc.

I have spoken with numerous audiences of employers or career counseling professionals who cite examples of Millennials asking for their offer letters to be sent to their parents instead of to them, parents coming along on job interviews, or networking events at which a parent will be asking question on behalf of their child and through the conversation the recruiter will come to realize that the adult child is actually standing right there. I have worries about what this infantilization can do to the development of self-esteem. As Dan Kindlon discusses in *Too Much of a Good Thing: Raising Children of Character in an Indulgent Age*, there is "the need for us to help our children to be psychologically self-sufficient. Only when they have a sense of self-efficacy can we feel confident that they will be able to persevere in the face of adversity and forge a life that is purposeful and vibrant."[14] If these seem like high concepts about what we hope to see in the rising generation, we need only remind ourselves of the far-reaching implications for someone who has not achieved this kind of self-efficacy. "Overinvolved parents do more than create havoc for school officials and coaches. They infantilize their children, creating dependent children who are stuck developmentally and are psychologically fragile. Their children are unable to manage everyday affairs. If they hit a minor speedbump – getting laid off from a job, as the economy almost continuously shifts – they often fall apart. ... They can't master the tasks of adulthood – and seem to have little inclination even to try. They are overly attached to their parents

---

[14] Dan Kindlon, Ph.D., *Too Much of a Good Thing: Raising Children of Character in an Indulgent Age* (New York: Hyperion, 2001).

and their parents to them."[15] And let's face it, on the most practical level, a job candidate who seems incapable of making a career decision without their parents' input may raise red flags for the prospective employer; these issues also suggest concern about the adult child's professionalism. The message that they are sending is that they aren't really capable of making adult decisions, and who wants an employee with that problem? Work is filled with daily decisions, and we all want employees who are confident and proficient in making them.

> *"[This is v]ery much frowned upon. It will never be accepted. It looks terrible. Helicopter parenting. It's terrible. Placating parents. Nothing is changing due to parents' involvement. Once you graduate you are an adult. Millennials like to extend childhood but enough is enough."*
> Alexandra Levitt
> Author, *How'd You Score That Gig*
> Millennial Workplace Consultant

But not everyone feels this way, and in fact many organizations are embracing the parental phenomena with vigor, and argue that this new level of involvement of parents with the work life of their adult children (especially when it is within reason) benefits the employee and the organization. The sentiment is that the employee will receive guidance from someone who knows them, cares about them, and is capable of helping them to make professional choices that are appropriate for them in the short and long term.

> *"I think this is a generation that is used to having support from parents, teachers, and friends, and this definitely plays out in the workplace as well. It's important for them to discuss their job offers and work issues with parents, stay in touch with mentors from college and high school, and even discuss salary with their peers. Therefore, it's imperative that we are aware of the support mechanisms that may help them stay with us as an employer of choice."*
> (cont. on page 30)

---

[15] Hara Estroff Marano, *A Nation of Wimps: The High Cost of Invasive Parenting* (New York: Broadway Books, 2008).

*(cont. from page 29)*

*"To anticipate this, we have put several support systems in place should the student need it. We've paired them with HR coaches, business mentors, 'buddies' that are in the same age range to help them navigate the cafeteria and fun places to go after work, and a slightly more senior peer to provide relevant career tips. I don't recall having this many support systems in place when I first started my career (and have to admit I'm a little jealous!) but it's simply the way it is and employers can choose to ignore it or use it to their advantage on finding great talent. We even have a parent's resource page on our career website to help parents research our company and access relevant information pertaining to our values and our mission. We try to put ourselves in the parent's shoes and think about what might be important for them to feel confident that we are the right place for a student to start a career."*

Helen Hong
College Relations Manager, WellPoint Inc.

It costs any organization a lot to recruit, hire, and train new employees, so if parental involvement in the front-end decision making about taking a particular job minimizes staff turnover, it advantages the organization as well as the new staff member.

*"Overprotective parents – those that won't let go – are an exception. Parents are much more involved. And it's a great thing. Kids know more about what they're getting into. They don't have to accept a terrible job offer. Parental involvement is a good thing. But that doesn't mean calling the interviewer, though many companies accommodate parental interest in other ways. Merrill Lynch sends out a letter to parents."*

Ryan Healy (Millennial) Co-Founder, Brazen Careerist

With all of the care and attention to their needs throughout their lives, Millennials have grown to have very high expectations, not just for themselves, but for others as well. The disappointment that I discuss is confined not just to missing out on the salary or promotion they desire, but also has to do with not having their needs met in the way that they expect. Remember, they are quite accustomed to a focus on their needs from the ultimate authority – their parents – and this sets a pretty high bar for authorities down the road, such as supervisors, with whom they often share a lot about themselves, even personal information. They have very high expectations for others and will lose trust in those who do not live up to those expectations. A result of this is that they often see others as being responsible for their experiences – beginning with their parents, and going on to include teachers, school administrators, and workplace managers – and they expect to be led. They also demand immediate results from their supervisor. If they ask for something, they expect to get it and they expect it right away.

> *"They expect thanks for things that are a part of their job. Other more mature staff think this is odd and unnecessary. They expect more than thanks; I'm not even sure what they want. We have not changed our ways, but would be interested in how to handle it."*
> Susan Shaer
> Executive Director, WAND
> (Women's Action for New Directions)

I have to say, this is not my experience of the professional world. Sure, there are times when I attain what I hope for in my professional life, including the guidance, promotion or raise, or even feedback, of which I am so desirous, but that is certainly not universally the case. Steve Kroft, a correspondent for the news show *60 Minutes*, did a story on "Echo Boomers" (another name for Millennials) in September of 2005, in which Millennials' pending experience with the workplace was discussed with Dr. Mel Levine, a professor at the University of North Carolina. When asked the question, "[w]hen a young person shows up at work today for their first job, what do they expect and what do they find?" Dr. Levine responded, "[t]hey expect to be immediate heroes and heroines. They expect a lot of feedback on a daily basis. They expect grade inflation. They expect to be told what a wonderful job they're doing. [They expect] that they're gonna be sort of allowed to rise to the top quickly, that they're gonna get all the credit they need for everything they do. And boy are they naïve. Totally naïve, in terms of what's really gonna happen."[16]

---

[16]  60 Minutes, "The Echo Boomers," September 4, 2005.

*"Yes, these employees need more guidance in dealing with workplace situations. In general they require more direction and appreciate guidelines when dealing with one another. They will work hard, but they need to be told exactly what their responsibilities are. When they need to work in groups, I have to assign the leader and distribute the tasks for them.*

*They also expect more consideration for their personal problems in the workplace. They will adjust their schedules, attitudes and outputs if they are dealing with a personal crisis and they think it is reasonable to expect a manager to be understanding. It feels like an erosion of professionalism whereby you present a pleasant front despite your personal life.*

*In general, there is more discussion about their personal lives. They are more willing to share details that I would have kept from my superiors. Interestingly this behavior has created a more collegial environment, which makes them more productive. It's a trade-off and right now we value the productivity more."*

Anonymous
Assistant Director
Career Development Non-Profit Organization

Not meeting these kinds of expectations can have a lot of implication for workplace satisfaction and, in turn, productivity and retention. A 2004 report from the Families and Work Institute cited that "[o]nly [Millennials] (18-22 in 2002) found fault with their supervisors, rating them somewhat lower than those of their own age in terms of overall competence and responsiveness to personal and family needs."[17] If this trend towards dissatisfaction with management's understanding of personal situations persists, Millennials may do a lot of job-changing to find a satisfactory environment, not something that any organization relishes. So then, **what can organizations do in the age of such significant parental involvement?** A major aspect involves accepting the role that parents have to play in the career decisions of their adult children.

---

[17] Families and Work Institute, *Generation and Gender in the Workplace*, (Families and Work Institute and The American Business Collaboration, 2004).

- **Career Development Seminars for parents.**

Colleges have been doing this for a little while now, to some success. Parents, especially given their financial investment in their child's education, want to know what the process is, what their kid should expect, and some of the most effective tactics and tools that their child can use to find that "perfect job." In a few cases, companies are starting to experiment with the employment of similar tools, and are also finding a bit of success with it. These parents are really partners on the job search process with their child – almost no matter what the age – so again this kind of outreach and information sharing can really help in successfully recruiting that top candidate.

> *"[I]n our company we have something called "Parents' Night" where we invite the Intern's parents to come to our corporate office and meet our company. They learn about what their child will be doing and how their experience will be beneficial. We introduce them to the College Unit Director and allow them to ask questions. This goes back to the family question. Family is a big deal. Also, our Managing Partner will send letters to the parents when their child achieves."*
> Becky Girola
> Director of Recruiting
> Northwestern Mutual Financial Network

- **Parent-Liaison Departments.**

This may be among the trends of the future. It began with high schools, especially prep schools, and then moved to the college level where we employee parent offices to aid in the growing demand for communication about our enrolled students, as well as to assist in partnering on individual student issues and larger programmatic efforts. There is movement and also potential opportunity, even as it requires some reframing, not just of practices, but of philosophical perspective as well, in capitalizing on parents' interest and involvement in their children's careers. Such offices can help to provide information to interested parents about company culture, the nature of their child's position, career progression opportunities, and answers to some basic questions around benefits and other organizational issues.

> *"Working in the Human Resources department, I deal with a lot of my Millennial employees wanting to consult their parents on different things such as what health insurance to pick, how to set up their 401K, etc. You don't know how many times I hear Millennials say that they need to ask their parents what their social security number is! On one occasion, I was making a job offer to a fellow Millennial and the candidate stated that she wasn't sure if she should accept the position and needed to talk to her father before she was allowed to take the job!"*
> Faryn Rosen (Millennial)
> Talent Acquisition Specialist, HR OnProcess Technology

Millennials and their parents alike are clamoring for this extra attention and service, and meeting these expectations can go a long way in building satisfaction. Remember, workplace satisfaction is a major issue for Millennials; given their relationships with their parents, this could be a great way to "kill two birds with one stone." Further, this concept could be expanded further and actually become a "Family-Liaison Department." Other employees, even Millennials as they get a bit older, may have established their own families, with partners and offspring, who may have questions or concerns about the company that they would like to discuss with an organizational representative. And as companies work to build employee satisfaction, even through events like family picnics or "bring your child to work day," there is no shortage of work to be done in a department such as this one.

- **Parent Newsletter.**
  Another way to connect with the parents of this generation, something that might be produced by the aforementioned Parent-Liaison Department, is a regular newsletter. This can be an excellent way to engage parents and provide them with information about what their child may experience in the organization, perhaps in a more general way while still keeping them somewhat at bay.

*"We realized that in order to get full buy-in from the students we needed to engage the parents in the process. We needed the parents to understand what we stand for and what this opportunity means. This past summer we sent three newsletters to parents highlighting different aspects of our program. This isn't summer camp, but the parents have invested a lot in these careers and we needed them on our side."*
Anonymous
Assistant Director
Career Development Non-Profit Organization

- **Enhance Training for Recruiters at Your Organization**

As I've discussed, there is a new trend here, one to which we must be reactive and responsive. No doubt, those in your Human Resources or Recruiting areas can tell you all about it, if you haven't yet been exposed to it yourself.

*["I] was recently at a seminar with 200 college recruiters. When asked if they had spoken with a parent in the actual recruiting process, at least 100 hands went up."*
Susan Kennedy
Job Coach
Career Treking

Those who are most likely to be exposed to concerned, and perhaps intervening, parents need to be equipped to address – or dismiss – questions from this audience. Not all issues are appropriate for anyone other than the job candidate/new employee, and more and more organizations are encountering the need to place limits on discussion. Some may need help with defining those limits, and finding ways to convey them without alienating what is clearly an important constituency.

*"I think that this 'Hover Parent' problem, where parents are calling and asking, 'what's wrong with John, why didn't you offer him the position,' is an overcompensation. The Hover Parent wants John to feel loved and supported, there is nothing wrong with that. It is the approach that is wrong."* (cont. on page 36)

*(cont. from page 35)*
*"When dealing with this group, it is important to handle with care. This relationship with this group can really be beneficial. Parents will be the buy-in, but as with any relationship, it is important to set boundaries. In HR we can let parents know that there are issues and situations that, legally, cannot be discussed with anyone but the party or parties directly involved. While we will try to answer any questions or assist with concerns, there are issues that we are not permitted to speak to."*
Cynthia Levinson
On-Site Supervisor at State Street Corporation
Kelly Complete

This gets into something that we at colleges have found ourselves doing for several years now, though we often wish we did not have to: teaching and counseling parents about the relationship that they need to develop as a parent of an "adult child." It is tough to offer what amounts to parenting advice to anyone, particularly a near-stranger, especially when the advice you want to offer suggests that they may be stifling their child's development. But guess what...you will increasingly find members of your organization placed in this situation.

*"If the calls are persistent from the same parent(s) then our recruiter will kindly offer the parent some advice and recommend that his/her son/daughter be calling with this question to build that relationship with the recruiter. We did incorporate a Parents' Day (family/friends day) in our internship program that was successful and we plan to enhance it for future programs. A committee of interns organized it and basically it was a lunch at our on-site cafeteria with other interns and parents, shopping at our Hallmark card shop on-site, a tour of the Hallmark visitor's center and a chance to meet coworkers and managers of their son/daughter's department."*
Julie Wille
College Recruiting Representative
Hallmark Cards

And even though you may not feel comfortable with overt statements of accessibility to parents regarding their adult children as employees at your organization, you can still provide information that will appeal to them and satisfy their questions and concerns without going farther than you wish to in inviting them into the "conversation."

> *"We have encountered isolated instances of direct contact with parents who are involved with their children's lives – wanting to help their child by making their travel arrangements to interviews, helping them to apply to opportunities. Although we aren't having too much direct contact with parents, we recognize that these students are much more inclined to discuss companies and packages with parents so we try to assure that our website, literature, and communication provide details that both might be interested in although we don't call out directly to parents in any of those mediums. We respect the parents' relationship with the child; however, we are clear that our primary customer is the candidate themselves."*
>
> Irene DeNigris
> Director, Global University Recruitment
> Johnson & Johnson

This is also a critical opportunity for the promotion of independence and self-efficacy for the Millennial employee or candidate.

> *"Each year we have a student information night in our office and students from area schools are invited. We had a young woman ask if her mother could attend the information night. We recognize that families are important; however, if someone becomes our employee we would expect to deal with them in all situations, not their parents. Consequently we said no to the young woman in order to promote a sense of independence to gather information about ones career aspirations. This is an isolated incident and not typical to most of the students we see."*
>
> Sarah Olson
> Director of Recruiting
> Berry, Dunn, McNeil & Parker, CPA

- **Mentoring New Employees**
  Despite the fact that there is much room for organizational growth and evolution in response to the major role that parents play with the Millennial Generation, I firmly believe that there is not just an opportunity

but really a desperate need to attend to the development of the Millennial employee with this issue. In *From B.A. to Payday*, Hayden and Wilder advise Millennials, "Helicopter Parents think they're doing what's best for you. They're not."[18] We need to teach our new Millennial employees how to be more decisive and convey self-efficacy and autonomy. So through intentional supervision and mentorship we effectively endeavor to retrain what more than two decades of parental influence has built.

> *"Millennials have been protected. They are the most child-centered period in history. They have been protected from disappointment. Their first setbacks and disappointments happen much later. Others experienced setbacks in high school or college – for Millennials, these first occur in the workplace.*
>
> *Millennials don't have the filter to be able to interpret. It is not necessarily that they are more emotional, but their backgrounds make it difficult to cope. Bosses are looked at [as] parental and authoritative. They do not know how to control their emotions.*
>
> *MENTORSHIP PROGRAMS are a huge part of this, formal and informal mentorship programs. Some groups like HR will set up an official process where an older colleague will pair with a younger colleague. It also provides opportunity for reverse mentoring and discussion around such issues as culture vs. technology, workplace issues, problems in the workplace. Informal programs [are] good for showing support. It's all about showing that you care, career development. [It] can't be faceless or they are going to leave. The traditional corporate environment is becoming more touchy-feely. Not all organizations are addressing the issue. They are spending much more time with 20-somethings. (Used to be Gen Y serving others, now it's the other way.) Bosses are parents, [and] have Millennials at homes – so they know how to deal with it. Though they have mixed feelings about it."*
>
> Alexandra Levitt, Author, *How'd You Score That Gig*
> Millennial Workplace Consultant

---

[18] D.A. Hayden and Michael Wilder, *From B.A. to Payday: Launching Your Career After College* (New York: Stewart, Tabori, & Chang: 2008).

Look, let's be real here. Of course parents are highly invested in their kids' lives, no matter how old they get. They've put their heart, soul, time, and money into giving them every bit of help that they possibly can. Parents have not only been told that this is what it means to be a parent, but they've also been constantly reminded of just how tough it is out there, how in today's dog-eat-dog world these advantages are key to survival, key not just to getting ahead, but to getting anywhere. And the Millennials are very in tune with their parents, often citing their value system as being fully aligned with their folks'. That was certainly not as much the case back in my day. Nor was it the case that I considered my parents, close as I may have been to them, to be my friends. In the *60 Minutes* report on the Echo Boomers, a group of about a dozen late teens were interviewed on camera and asked if they were close to their parents. As the heads bobbed up and down in enthusiastic agreement, several could be heard saying "yes, they're my best friends," and "don't want to leave them."[19] Even if I did feel that way at 17 or 18, it was certainly not "socially acceptable" to say so in a room full of my peers. But times have changed, and Millennials and their parents are connected on levels that Gen X-ers and Boomers were not, so parents remain a very active part of their children's lives even as they reach adulthood, even in their professional lives.

Many companies are quite comfortable with a reasonable level of involvement from parents, and even find that they are able to exploit this to their advantage, particularly in the hiring process.

*"What I do see is [M]illennials conferring with their parents about the offers they receive. I think this is great. I want a new hire to come in to our organization understanding as much as they can about their offer, benefits and opportunities. Their parents are a great resource in this situation. However, we will only discuss things pertaining to an employee/applicant with that employee/ applicant. These are private and personal matters between the organization and the employee/applicant and should not be discussed with anyone else. We do not share personal information of our employees with their parents."*
Matt Duren
College Recruiting Manager
GEICO

---

[19] 60 Minutes, "The Echo Boomers," September 4, 2005.

Really it's no wonder we see a generation of young adults who have been formed – in good ways and bad – by the experience of an upbringing by ultra-involved parents. And we do our best to advise them in ways that help them to grow as self-sufficient adults fully capable of making personal and professional decisions. But we also must adjust to the massive ongoing influence of parents – Helicopter or not – in the lives of their adult children. They have borne this power and authority for more than 20 years, and it and they aren't going anywhere. After all, Millennials may be "The Hovered Generation."

# CHAPTER ONE: SUMMARY

- Millennials are sheltered; they have very close relationships with their families, and feel truly supported, but they have little experience figuring things out for themselves.

- Millennials and their families often perpetuate a sense of arrested development long after they reach young adulthood.

- The "overly involved" parents of Millennials have become known – with some controversy – as "Helicopter Parents," due to their perceived near-constant hovering. Technology continues to be a major enabler of this deep and ongoing connection between the Millennial generation, as college students and as young new professionals, and their parents.

- Millennials struggle with disappointment, as they have in many cases been sheltered from such experiences throughout their formative years, and the "lack of practice" with this has led to deficient coping skills.

- More and more employers and career counseling professionals are experiencing incidences of Millennials asking for their offer letters to be sent to their parents instead of to them, parents coming along on job interviews, or parents speaking on behalf of their adult children at professional networking events. This suggests an infantilization of the Millennials that may have a negative impact on the development of self-esteem and self-efficacy. This also sends concerning messages to prospective employers – that the Millennial job candidate is not really capable of making adult decisions.

- Millennials have become accustomed to the focus on their needs that has been established by their parents, and this has in turn established a pattern of expectation for subsequent authorities down the road, such as supervisors. Millennials have very high expectations for others and will lose trust in those who do not live up to those expectations. They also demand immediate results from their supervisors.

- Organizations can react to these dynamics with the development of Career Development Seminars for parents, Parent-Liaison Departments, parent newsletters, the enhancement of training for recruiters at the organization, and mentorship programs for new employees.

# CHAPTER TWO

## Millennials - Generation R$_x$?

Very recently, I was at a conference where a colleague of mine from another college told the audience that 75 percent of the female and 80 percent of the male students at her school have disclosed that they take some form of prescription medication. This represents much higher numbers than we have seen in previous generations of college students. I think that this particular school may be an outlier in this regard, but the fact is that much of the data we have on Millennials and overall mental health is actually a bit concerning.

Now, we cannot forget that these drugs include pharmaceutical treatment for learning disabilities, such as Ritalin or other treatments for Attention Deficit Hyperactive Disorder (ADHD), as well as for other mental health ailments, such as depression, bipolarism, etc. Apparently, over twenty-one million prescriptions are written yearly for drugs designed to enhance attention span in children – ages 6 to 14. This is an increase of over 400 percent in the past decade; during this same time, antidepressant use in children of this same age range has increased by 333 percent.[20]

The Society for College and University Planning (SCUP) produces a bi-annual report on "Trends to Watch in Higher Education;" the August 2008 report addressed, amidst its discussion of changing demographics in higher education as a trend of import, that the number one issue related to changing demographics is the rise in mental health concerns amongst college students. "The mental health of students attending college is increasingly becoming a cause for concern, in both the US and Canada. The number of students who seek and need mental health services is only likely to rise. Increased awareness and decreased stigmatization for treatment

---

[20] Hara Estroff Marano, *A Nation of Wimps: The High Cost of Invasive Parenting* (New York: Broadway Books, 2008).

contribute to this trend, but don't explain it all."[21] Citing studies by the American College Health Association—National College Health Assessment and the National Survey of Counseling Center Directors 2007, SCUP discusses a college-age population that is reporting more depression, anxiety, and major psychological disorders.

Of course, we cannot dismiss the fact that college students, both due to the developmental phase of life that they are in (particularly if they are of traditional college age of approximately 18 to 22) and the highly charged environment in which they exist, experience their life occurrences in what may be a more deeply affecting way. Dr. Richard Kadison and Theresa Foy DiGeronimo, in their book *College of the Overwhelmed: The Campus Mental Health Crisis and What To Do About It*, point out that "[l]ate adolescence is a time of transition, a period of reflection on family values, career aspirations, and lifestyle experimentation. ... Part of the function of college is to give young adults the freedom to explore their world. ... And although this is a normal developmental process, it is a source of great anxiety for many college students."[22] I have worked with college students for long enough to realize that the transition to the new environment, the exposure to new ideas, and the fast-paced growth and development that occurs between the formative phases of late adolescence and early adulthood can throw them for quite a loop. Many students grapple with new ideas about their family, their relationships, and their goals, and this can cause significant emotional turmoil. The point is, much of this is normal developmental challenges. The problem is, that is not the whole picture.

For example, I am fascinated by the fact that the SCUP "Trends to Watch in Higher Education" report discusses mental health as a demographic issue. It is very telling that what was once considered to be a more individualized issue is now being considered as a demographic concern... and the top demographic concern at that. When did mental health become a demographic issue? And what does it mean for the aspects of society outside of our college campuses and their gates? The fact that mental health is being considered in this way by our institutions of higher educa-

---

[21] Society for College and University Planning, *Trends in Higher Education*, August 2008, 10/18/08 [http://www.scup.org/pdf/SCUP_Trends_8-2008.pdf].

[22] Richard Kadison, MD and Theresa Foy DiGeronimo
*College of the Overwhelmed: The Campus Mental Health Crisis and What To Do About It*, (California: Jossey-Bass, 2004).

tion certainly suggests that it will play a substantially larger role in other functional areas of society; companies will have to consider this issue as it relates to the ways in which they work with their employees.

On college campuses we have seen the psychological issues manifest in many ways. While it is generally the "sensational" issues that hit the media and draw tremendous attention, such as major catastrophes like the mass-shootings at Virginia Tech or Northern Illinois University, our nation's colleges and universities are struggling with a myriad of mental health issues amongst the collective student body. I and my colleagues often wonder to one another if we have become clinical care environments or are still educational institutions. As Marano discusses in *A Nation of Wimps*, "[c]ollege is where the fragility factor is having its greatest impact. By all accounts, psychological distress is rampant on college campuses. The young are breaking down in record numbers and showing serious forms of distress in ways previous generations did not."[23]

A 2006 survey conducted by the American College Health Association cites that just over of 35 percent of students had reported experiencing "feeling so depressed it was difficult to function" between one and ten times in the past year, and 6.7 percent had experienced that level of depression more than 11 times during the year. Moreover, almost 13 percent reported experiencing significant anxiety disorder.[24] While stress and feelings of being overwhelmed are common to and expected of college students, it is somewhat alarming that nearly 30 percent of college students described "feeling overwhelmed by all that they had to do" more than 11 times in the past year.[25] Perhaps more concerning is that 8.5 percent of the students reported "seriously considering attempting suicide" anywhere from one to ten times over the past year, with .9 percent seriously considering it 11 or more times.[26] As the SCUP report states, "[a] poll conducted

---

[23] Hara Estroff Marano, *A Nation of Wimps: The High Cost of Invasive Parenting* (New York: Broadway Books, 2008).

[24] American College Health Association, *National College Health Assessment: Reference Group Executive Summary*, Fall 2006, 12/24/08 [http://www.isu.edu/wellness/pdf/ACHA-NCHA_Reference_Group_ExecutiveSummary_Fall2006.pdf].

[25] Ibid.

[26] Ibid.

in March 2008 of 2,253 undergraduates at four-year institutions indicated that 80 percent of students said they felt stressed. They reported that 16 percent of their friends had talked about suicide and 11 percent had made an attempt. Over a quarter of the respondents had considered talking to a mental health professional since starting school."[27]

All college students are at risk of minor and major mental health concerns, and in fact, colleges are dealing with the demands of unprecedented numbers of students with a wide range of issues, from the more minor and less significant to the very serious and often increasingly complex psychological disorders. Though some of these students may experience difficulty meeting their academic demands, and consequently under perform in their coursework, many continue to excel academically and pre-professionally despite the issues with which they are dealing. However, it is not without a cost to the individual and to the college. According to the SCUP Report, over 90 percent of campus counseling center directors report that the recent trend toward greater numbers of students with severe psychological problems exists on their campuses.[28] This creates a heavy burden for college campuses in supporting students to achieve their academic and professional goals.

One might assume that the students struggling in this way are not our most achieving young minds of this generation, and thus perhaps not the students who you may be hoping to recruit to work at your organization. That assumption would be wrong. In fact, anecdotally speaking, we find it is sometimes the highest achieving students, under great personal and familial pressure to succeed, who experience the most significant consequences of stress and depression. Young people worry more than ever about their future; we, in turn, worry about what this does to them. It is great that they have drive and determination, but their stress affects them physically. Studies show that many have never learned how to create balance in life and, as a consequence, have trouble sleeping and maintaining a reasonable schedule, staying healthy, and dealing with the normal hurdles of life. Their stress level makes them more prone to anxiety and other emotional concerns, essentially more fragile.

---

[27] Society for College and University Planning, *Trends in Higher Education*, August 2008, 10/18/08 [http://www.scup.org/pdf/SCUP_Trends_8-2008.pdf].

[28] Ibid.

In fact, in a study released by Kansas State University in March 2003, a research team led by psychologist Sherry Benton, discovered a tremendous rise in students seeking psychological support and treatment for stress and anxiety issues in particular. As discussed in an article by Karen Patterson for the *Dallas Morning News*, who interviewed Benton regarding these findings, "[t]roubles with dating and other relationships were the most frequently reported issue among students seeking counseling until 1994, when stress and anxiety problems surpassed them. From 1988 to 1992, about 36 percent had stress or anxiety issues, compared with almost 47 percent who had relationship problems. But from 1996 to 2001, almost 63 percent of the students had stress and anxiety problems, and about 56 percent relationship problems. While it's not surprising that 18- to 24-year-olds would struggle with relationships, Benton said, 'you don't really expect stress and anxiety.'"[29] College students for many years now have sought counseling support for the issues that they face in their everyday lives, but the surge in stress-related issues is a very compelling and concerning situation for psychologists like Benton, college administrators such as myself, and the prospective employers of these soon-to-be-graduates.

Let's be careful here. First of all, college is, for most, a wonderful time of life, in which the dearest lifelong friends can be made, tremendous intellectual growth and curiosity is enabled, and long-term professional goals are established and embarked upon. But we know that all of this can be quite overwhelming for some, and, as I have discussed, more and more students are coming to college with significant personal and emotional issues even before they undergo this challenging developmental stage. On top of that, colleges and parents have set a pretty high baseline standard of support for these young people. I'll be frank: I am not sure I'd have it any other way, but it comes with some cost to the younger generation. Would we leave a student undergoing a struggle to "figure it out" by themselves without our guidance and support? Of course not. That would unacceptable by any standard, to the students, their families, or us.

At the overwhelming majority of college campuses, we have established a multitude of services designed to support our students through not just academic struggles, but also personal ones. Most schools offer a

---

[29] Karen Patterson, "Counseling Study Paints Picture of Heavier College Woes; More Students Seen with Depression, Suicidal Thoughts," *Dallas Morning News*, February 10, 2003.

myriad of services for personal support through student affairs and residential life, counseling services, the significant availability of faculty and other administrators, leadership development programs, spiritual life, and wellness programs and fitness centers. These are designed to help students not just with their transition to the college environment, but to also aid in any issues that may arise along the way. And many issues do arise. Colleges have acknowledged that in our mission to educate students, there is a lot more work that often needs to be done to provide them with the personal resources that they need to succeed academically. Also in this picture are the parents, with whom colleges partner – whenever possible – on an as-needed basis to support students through their trials and tribulations.

Thus there really are a lot of people working with and on behalf of students to assist them through their challenges and feelings of being overwhelmed. As I said, I think this is a good thing, but I also see the issues that may develop from it. Ideally these support systems are helping students to develop their own lifelong coping mechanisms, so that they have the ability to face the personal and professional challenges that we all know exist in the world of adulthood. But is this always the case? I would argue that some of the handholding that we as a collective society, have done is keeping young people from developing the coping mechanisms that they need. Too much is done to minimize their discomfort and solve their problems.

*"As for our 'organization', we seem to have wrapped our services around the students and created a service cocoon. It has been highly incremental, but I have watched it grow in scope for 25 years. I know we think we are providing advice and comfort at key points in their social and academic lives, but maybe it's too much? Look, for example, at the [transition to college] program. There's virtually no intellectual content in this 'seminar'...it's really just an extended orientation that goes on and on and on. And yet I've been in many meetings during which the need for this is broadly supported because we think they need to be continually fed information or they'll make some huge error in their career planning. Interesting that our response as an institution may be reinforcing [M]illennial behaviors."*
Anonymous
College Professor

Colleges, and parents too, for that matter, are oft debating the question "what should be done?" and "how much is enough?" Colleges are most concerned with the development of the student, not simply academically and with direct correlation to their learning in the classes in which they are enrolled, but also overall, with their growth towards full and self-sustaining adulthood. The kind of care that colleges provide around mental health issues is essential and can and should contribute to the students' overall development, but only if it helps them to learn the processing and coping skills that build their capacity to manage stress and anxiety. These stressors do not go away, and often are exacerbated as Millennials reach the workplace environment. As Millennials graduate from college and take jobs in various organizations, they will continue to face personal and professional stressors, and will now face them without easy access to the resources that are typical on most of today's college campuses. In fact, many of the anxiety issues that impact their personal and academic lives as students will have similar impact on their lives as professional in the workplace.

*"I do notice that I'm dealing with more people with anxiety and crying at work."*
Roger F. Prahl
Lawyer
Litigation Services

So while this is interesting and no doubt distressing information to us all, why is such an extensive discussion of what we are seeing on college campuses relevant to the employer? These issues are unlikely to end as students graduate from college. In fact, the National Institute of Mental Health (NIMH) reports that 'Major Depressive Disorder' is the leading cause of disability in the U.S. for ages 15 through 44, and that it affects approximately 14.8 million American adults, or about 6.7 percent of the U.S. population age 18 and older in a given year.[30] The statistics about anxiety are even more concerning: according to the NIMH, approximately 40 million American adults ages 18 and older, or about 18.1 percent of people in this age group, have an anxiety disorder. Anxiety disorders can include panic disorder, obsessive-compulsive disorder, post-traumatic stress dis-

---

[30] National Institute of Mental Health, "The Numbers Count: Mental Disorders in America," [http://www.nimh.nih.gov/health/publications/the-numbers-count-mental-disorders-in-america.shtml#MajorDepressive].

order, generalized anxiety disorder, and phobias.[31] Both depression and anxiety generally manifest themselves in feelings of being overwhelmed and beleaguered.

> *"I have one intern right now who exhibits this anxiety and stress. The reason is clearly because she is very pressured by her parents to be perfect. She is a grad student because they told her that she had to go to grad school. If she misses a task or works less-than-normal hours, she is very disappointed in herself. She is one of the greatest interns we have, so she seems very hard on herself, for the great job she is doing."*
> Ashley Humphrey
> Director of Internship Program
> ExamOne, a Quest Diagnostics subsidiary

In an issue brief prepared by the Families and Work Institute (FWI) for the American Business Collaboration (ABC), which explored generation and gender, beginning with a focus on younger employees, it was found that "college-educated Gen-Y [Millennial] employees who more often feel 'overwhelmed by how much they have to do on their jobs' are much less likely to want jobs with greater responsibility."[32] When the data for this study was collected in 2002, these members of the Millennial Generation were between 18 and 22. It is important to note that the same sentiment was found amongst Gen-X (ages 23 through 37 years at the time of data collection) and Boomer employees (ages 38 through 57 years at the time of data collection); however, the difficulty in dealing with stress and anxiety is believed by some – though not all – to be pandemic to the Millennial generation, whereas these previous generations are not typified by this psychographic characteristic in the same way.

---

[31] National Institute of Mental Health, "The Numbers Count: Mental Disorders in America," [http://www.nimh.nih.gov/health/publications/the-numbers-count-mental-disorders-in-america.shtml#Anxiety].

[32] Families and Work Institute, *Generation and Gender in the Workplace*, (Families and Work Institute and The American Business Collaboration, 2004).

> *"I think the environment is different today than it was with other generations, and it is unfair to judge the group's ability to cope against another generations'. I believe Millennials, for the most part, are a resilient group driven to succeed. They may process their feelings a bit more verbally than their stoic elders, but I think that people who complain about the Millennials are out of touch with the things they did at that age."*
> Seth Nable
> Manager, Training and Development
> Human Resources OnProcess Technology

I have a strong reaction to this; it causes me to ponder whether Millennials, due to what may be a heightened sense of fragility, are less likely to want to take on professional roles with higher pressure. The Families and Work Institute asked the question "[d]o the generations differ in their desire to advance?" and found that the most dramatic decline is seen with the Millennial generation. In 1992, 80 percent of employees under 23 years of age (late Gen X-ers) aspired to jobs with more responsibility; in 2002, with employees under 23 years of age (early Millennials), that proportion had dropped to 60 percent, a decline of 20 percentage points.[33] While this may be attributable to a variety of factors, the survey goes on to present a direct link, citing that "employees who more frequently feel overwhelmed by all they have to do at work are less likely to want jobs with greater responsibility."[34] This could be described as a concerning decline in ambition among the Millennial Generation. Remember, Millennials are a generation that have been brought up with great ambition and strong messaging – from their families and from society – about the need for ambition and success. So when we see that a clear psychography of difficulty managing stress and anxiety leading towards a possible downward trend in ambition, we need to consider this. What can organizations do? What resources can be put in place to assist employees around issues of stress? Just as colleges have reacted to the mental health trend, one that the Society for College and University Planning calls a demographic issue, so must companies and other workplace organizations. If it truly a demographic issue, then the situation will undoubtedly continue to persist.

---

[33] Ibid.

[34] Ibid.

It is also important to consider the rise in documented learning disabilities amongst the Millennial Generation and the history of academic (and other) accommodations that these students have received throughout their lives, as well as the increase in medication use for Millennials. The impact of this has been felt over the years in many venues, as discussed in a 2006 *New York Times* article about the changing role of camp nurses: "A quick gulp of water, a greeting from the nurse, and the youngsters move on to the next table for orange juice, Special K and chocolate chip pancakes. The dispensing of pills and pancakes is over in minutes, all part of a typical day at a typical sleep-away camp in the Catskills. The medication lines like the one at Camp Echo were unheard of a generation ago but have become fixtures at residential camps across the country. Between a quarter and half of the youngsters at any given summer camp take daily prescription medications, experts say. Allergy and asthma drugs top the list, but behavior management and psychiatric medications are now so common that nurses who dispense them no longer try to avoid stigma by pretending they are vitamins. ... 'This is the American standard now,' said Rodger Popkin, an owner of Blue Stars Camps in Hendersonville, N.C. 'It's not limited by education level, race, socioeconomics, geography, gender or any of those filters.'"[35] While I doubt that company dispensaries (if they even still exist) will be charged with managing various medications of this type to employees – although I guess you never know – I do acknowledge that the experience with medication and with accommodations likely has bearing on work life. Many of these employees in question are accustomed to extra time on exams, reduced-distraction testing environments, and other adjustments. I am not sure that these are always possible in the work setting, and it will be interesting to see what they mean for Millennial employees with this history.

I made the argument earlier that we have already done a lot as a society to foster an expectation of care and resources in the college environment, an expectation that may not be unreasonable but certainly perpetuates a reliance on such hand-holding amongst the Millennial Generation. I don't lay blame on our colleges and universities; how can I? I am a part of that system! I think that students, their parents, and our society have asked this of us. And now, that train is moving – and we have only fed the need. So then we send our graduates off to work with you, and they are used to this. They expect this. And you want to have employees who are as effec-

---

[35] Jane Gross, "Checklist for Camp: Bug Spray. Sunscreen. Pills." *New York Times*, July 16, 2006.

tive and productive as possible. This relies to a large degree upon them being able to manage their emotional and psychological lives. They need to be "okay" in order to perform at their jobs to the level that you desire, and while you may hold no responsibility to help them to be "okay," you certainly benefit significantly when they are.

> *"I do believe that I have more personal issues and emotional concerns that are brought to work. I'm not always prepared for certain situations and I find myself getting stressed out easily and sometimes my anxiety gets so bad that I break down in front of my co-workers. On more than one occasion I've cried at work, which in retrospect is really embarrassing. It's funny because on a few different occasions, when I'm in the midst of having a bad day, I've actually called my family from my desk at work to vent. I do believe that my [M]illennial peers and I need more guidance on how to deal with stressful workplace issues. I think that in our organization the leadership group offers my [M]illennial peers and me opportunities to discuss and vent about our workplace issues, as well as help each other figure out other ways to deal with tough situations in the workplace. I also don't think that it is necessarily an employer's responsibility to make sure that every employee is able to cope with tough situations. We have a Human Resources department that offers some help and guidance as well. Between all the programs that were mentioned, I think that that is all that should be expected of an employer."*
>
> Faryn Rosen (Millennial)
> Talent Acquisition Specialist, Human Resources OnProcess Technology

Given that we believe Millennials to have a propensity towards stress and anxiety issues, and we also know why you want them to be able to deal with that anxiety, what can you do about it? Obviously, you can't go back and rewire them so that the entire generation does not have a predilection toward these issues; if we could, we at the colleges would have tried it already! I suggest that this is not about proaction, but really about reaction. You are bringing a new generation to your workforce that not only needs, but now expects, resources and services to make them feel better about their experience. And you need for them to feel that way, as it makes them more productive and contributory. *So, the million dollar question: what do you do?*

- **Flexibility in the work environment.**

The Families and Work Institute reports in the *Generation and Gender in the Workplace* brief that "employees with access to flexibility are more likely to be engaged and committed, to be satisfied with their jobs, to want to remain with their employers, and to have better mental health."[36] As Jean Twenge discusses in *Generation Me*, "[t]oday's young people also appreciate flexible schedules and independence. They don't respond well to micromanagement, and will find rigid schedules stifling. ... GenMe loves doing their own thing and will like working at a place that values this."[37] Clearly, there is a lot to be said for a flexible work environment. This is particularly important for women, particularly those who are mothers or are considering parenthood. I believe this concern is there for all parents and prospective parents, but, as of this writing, I maintain that the challenge of home-work balance is still more of one for women parents than it is for men.

- **Technology can aid in providing flexibility.**

Millennials are more tech-savvy than any generation that has preceded them, and can often utilize technology in order to work from anywhere. Providing the opportunity for alternate work environments, telecommuting programs, and the like is a great way to proffer flexibility to employees without reducing either productivity or an organization's expectation of its employees.

> *"We've found that the Millennial Generation is much more accepting of non-traditional work environments than established businesses care to recognize. Millennials simply embrace experiential, mobile and highly-engaging work over the opposite. Additionally, Millennials are inherently mobile workers equipped with top-notch laptops and communication devices – oftentimes better equipment than a company can provide – and they are quite adept at using the technology as well. They've spent years in college working in a social and dynamic environment and are finding that 'traditional' work environments aren't as suitable to optimizing their productivity as they desire."* (cont. on page 55)

---

[36] Families and Work Institute, *Generation and Gender in the Workplace*, (Families and Work Institute and the American Business Collaboration, 2004).

[37] Jean M. Twenge, PhD, *Generation Me: Why Today's Young Americans Are More Confident, Assertive, Entitled – and More Miserable Than Ever Before* (New York: Free Press, 2006).

> *(cont. from page 54)*
> *"Hence, they gravitate to work environments that are increasingly more non-traditional. Companies that embrace these traits of new workers will be better positioned for the future than those who labor to make Millennials fit into traditional roles, cubicles and structure."*
> Mason Gates, President, Internships.com

In fact, an article in the *Boston Globe Magazine* from July 20, 2008 discussed several companies, experiment with unlimited vacation time. While companies were originally concerned with abuses to this generous policy, they found that the exact opposite occurred. "Depending on your perspective, Steve Swasey is either an oppressed worker or the luckiest guy in the world. As a salaried employee at video-rental giant Netflix, Swasey has no set number of vacation days. He can spend as much time out of his California office as he wants, provided, of course, that he gets all his work done. And there's the hitch: Like many of today's competitive profession-als, Swasey always has more work that he could do."[38] This became the new concern: that even when officially on vacation, employees would find themselves spending on average at least an hour a day doing work. And while this can – and certainly does – lend itself to employees experiencing feelings of being overwhelmed by what they have to do for their job, the overall sense of workplace flexibility continues to have the positive influ-ences, though mixed with the obvious negatives cited in the *Generation and Gender in the Workplace* brief.

> *"Millennials are much more efficient in how they get work done. They can leverage technology to get things done faster. [They are used to i]nterruptions like IM, cell phone, text [and are c]riticized most for Blackberry's at meetings. Companies provide Millennials with access to technology. [The p]ercentage of face time in [the] office is much lower. Employees can work anytime, anywhere. Mil-lennials are leading the charge to come in later. Companies lessen expectations to always hang around the office. [We will c]ontinue to see [this] in the coming years. [It is the t]ip of the iceberg for now."* Alexandra Levitt, Author, *How'd You Score That Gig*
> Millennial Workplace Consultant

---

[38] Alison Lobron, "Is Unlimited Vacation a Good Thing?," *Boston Globe Magazine* July, 20, 2008.

- **Teamwork should be utilized to enhance flexibility.**

Millennials have tremendous experience with teaming, and this is something that can provide the flexibility that can be advantageous as well. The sharing of projects allows for employees to manage peak times with responsibilities in a way that simultaneously provides some control over workload and workplace stress. "Understand that teamwork is king – Millennials have been working in teams their whole lives. While Gen X-ers may visibly recoil at having to go to yet another meeting about a task force convened for a project, the team dynamic is second nature to Millennials. Millennials will value opportunities to work in groups with not only peers, but colleagues across departments and divisions. Make time for meetings and group work, and ensure that the Millennials you manage are exposed to teamwork often."[39]

> *"We have a very collaborative environment so it is a great asset to have employees who are open to collaborative working environments. We do work independently, as well; I think some staff have a hard time moving things forward without a team cheering them on. It seems we have more requests for project management training now, which we plan to implement."*
> Anonymous
> HR Business Partner, Multimedia Publishing Company

Of course, there is a downside to all this teamwork and its intersection with workplace stress. Many Millennial (and other generation) workers experience the anxiety of responsibility for projects for which they are not the sole owner. Sharing responsibility for a major deliverable means that the control does not rest entirely in your hands, and this can be a very challenging notion for some employees. This is something that requires careful supervision and management.

---

[39] Maureen Crawford Hentz, "Managing Millennials," *NEHRA – The Voice of HR*, The Northeast Human Resources Association, June 11, 2007, 12/3/08 [http://www.boston.com/jobs/nehra/061107.shtml].

*"Most of our more entry-level positions require teamwork. The difficulty is that project-based work has two evaluations, the project['s] successful completion and the individual contributor performance. We have not changed our ways of working as a result of this. We use our standard quality process and try to work with the employees on the issues where they fall short of the expectation."*
Cynthia Levinson
On-Site Supervisor at State Street Corporation
Kelly Complete

- **Generous benefits and programs for employees.**

Today's young employees have very high expectations of what perks and services will be available to them through their workplace. They are accustomed to the myriad of services that they have received through their academic and societal settings leading up to this point, and of course in their eyes this should not change. According to *What Millennial Workers Want*, "[n]early three-quarters (73%) of Gen Y professionals are concerned about being able to balance a career with personal obligations. You'll encourage longer tenures and greater loyalties among employees if you offer perks and programs that help them achieve work/life balance. This may require you to rethink traditional career paths or timetables for advancement, or offer options such as job-sharing, telecommuting, compressed workweeks, or alternative scheduling, where appropriate."[40] The more support that exists in the workplace that enables healthy work-life balance, the better Millennials will be able to manage their stress and anxiety, which will of course positively influence their productivity, retention, and advancement. "With so many more dual-income families, perks like on-site day care, flexible schedules, work-at-home options, and generous parental leave policies will also significantly improve retention."[41]

---

[40] Robert Half International and YAHOO! Hot Jobs, "What Millennial Workers Want: How to Attract and Retain Gen Y Employees," (California, 2007).

[41] Jean M. Twenge, PhD, *Generation Me: Why Today's Young Americans Are More Confident, Assertive, Entitled – and More Miserable Than Ever Before*, (New York: Free Press, 2006).

> *"Some of the things these folks worry about or get stressed about seem minute in the big scheme of things. But I think that is generally a maturity thing. I have not seen a big change in this area recently. We have had more requests for EAP assistance, [and] benefits going to more mental health prescriptions and services."*
> Anonymous
> HR Business Partner
> Multimedia Publishing Company

• **Employee Assistance Programs.**

Employee assistance programs are not a new phenomenon, but one for which there is a greater need than ever before. According to the "EAPA Standards and Professional Guidelines for Employee Assistance Programs" published by the Employee Assistance Professionals Association, "the 'Employee Assistance Program' or 'EAP' is a worksite-based program designed to assist: (1) work organizations in addressing productivity issues, and (2) 'employee clients' in identifying and resolving personal concerns, including, but not limited to, health, marital, family, financial, alcohol, drug, legal, emotional, stress, or other personal issues that may affect job performance … [representing] the essential components of the employee assistance (EA) profession. These components combine to create a unique approach to addressing work-organization productivity issues and 'employee client' personal concerns affecting job performance and ability to perform on the job."[42]

> *"Within Johnson & Johnson we have wonderful services for all employees to help them cope with stress and balancing work and family. A program we instituted several years ago is called Life 360 and it includes programs like: Financial & Retirement Planning, Health & Benefits including wellness & fitness, flexible work plans, programs around Family changes including counseling, Elder Care Services, Child Care and parenting services."*
> Irene DeNigris
> Director, Global University Recruitment
> Johnson & Johnson

---

[42] Employee Assistance Professionals Association,
"EAPA Standards and Professional Guidelines for Employee Assistance Programs,"
2003, 12/12/08
[http://www.eapassn.org/public/articles/EAPA_STANDARDS_web0303.pdf].

Offerings through an Employee Assistance Program might include coaching programs around the issues of separation of personal and professional life. This is not a challenge unique to Millennials, though perhaps more significant for them than for other generations, and thus could be a useful resource for all employees. In general, this is also an area where the generation gap, in action and understanding, is quite substantial.

*"It seems like they have limited coping skills for work, family and relationships and they all blend together. Troubles bleed into the workplace and there are no boundaries. They expect their problems to be of interest to everyone and if it affects their work, that's just the way it is. They don't understand the concept of keeping their personal troubles at the door. Our organization is very family friendly, but some boundaries should be kept. It's a soft line in our group, and even harder with the new generation.*

*They do not seem to expect nor care that mature workers have wisdom. They do not honor older people of substance or notoriety; they don't seem to care. They have been told they are equals and they act like equals.*

*They expect their ideas to be heralded. If it isn't, they are hurt and consider the less than positive reaction just wrong. It never occurs to them that someone else has had that idea before, or that they should listen more and learn more before they jump in. I'm not suggesting they should be silent; but respectful. And they never seem to think that's necessary.*

*We only have 15 employees, so we don't have an institutional way to deal with this. We have considered ageism training. And we do include everyone in all staff meetings and request all to participate and offer suggestions. We think everyone should offer ideas."*

Susan Shaer
Executive Director, WAND
(Women's Action for New Directions)

This chapter has discussed at great length the emotional and psychological issues that face the Millennial generation, issues that are not likely to go anywhere as they hit the work environment. More and more companies are finding that the utilization of concrete programs to aid their employees in managing the demands of work and life benefit the organization overall. Furthermore, employees are not shy in asking for these kinds of resources.

*"I don't particularly think [Millennials'] issues are any worse than other associates', I just think they are different. I do think they are more vocal about their concerns and don't think about it looking particularly 'bad' in the eyes of others. Since their whole lives they've been encouraged to express their concerns, they naturally assume that it's okay to do that in the workplace. It's a definite shift in communications for many of our current associates because some of them come from the mindset of veering away from conversations that may be seen as negative. Truthfully, when they are able to discuss their concerns and find ways to resolve it, they are actually more committed to the organization because they are then fully engaged. I think it's an advantage that the student has so many support systems outside of work because that helps them deal with the pressures of the workplace by providing sounding boards for their thoughts. We benefit as an employer because they have strong emotional support from family and their peers acknowledge that they're not alone."*
Helen Hong
College Relations Manager
WellPoint Inc.

Millennials, with all that they have to offer to the workplace, are clearly at their best when their emotional and psychological needs are being met. They have come to expect this and, I might say, even to need this. Many of the programs discussed in this chapter are not new to the world of business, as they have been employed in a variety of work settings over the years, but what we are seeing now is a greater need and a greater benefit to their utilization in this day of "Generation $R_x$."

## CHAPTER TWO: SUMMARY

• Much of the data that we have on Millennials and overall mental health is fairly concerning. The Society for College and University Planning produces a bi-annual report on "Trends to Watch in Higher Education;" the August 2008 report addressed that the number one issue related to changing demographics is the rise in mental health concerns amongst college students.

• There has been a dramatic surge in anxiety and stress-related issues for college students in recent years, and this is considered a compelling and concerning situation for psychologists, college administrators and faculty, and the prospective employers of the soon-to-be-graduates.

• As Millennials graduate from college and take on professional roles, they will continue to face personal and professional stressors, and will now face them without the easy access to the resources that is typical on most of today's college campuses. In fact, many of the anxiety issues that impact their personal and academic lives as students will have similar impact on their lives as professionals in the workplace.

• There is data that suggests Millennials, due to what may be a heightened sense of fragility, are less likely to want to take on professional roles with higher pressure.

• There has been a rise in documented learning disabilities amongst the Millennial Generation and a subsequent history of academic (and other) accommodations that these students have received, as well as the increase in medication usage for Millennials. Many companies will see new employees who are accustomed to extra time on exams, reduced distraction testing environments, and other adjustments, and this may have impact on their workplace needs and expectations.

• Organizations may find that in order for their employees to be as productive as possible in the workplace, they need to be responsive to these mental health issues and other related matters. Effective responses may include providing more flexibility in the work environment, by utilizing technology to allow employees to work more from home, and employing team-based approaches to project management. Other useful tools in addressing staff satisfaction with work environments can include the implementation of generous benefits and professional development programs, and Employee Assistance Programs.

# CHAPTER THREE

## Millennials - 2.0?

*"On Sunday, October 26th, I decided to put away my iPod, cellular phone, laptop and other devices which pretty much make up my life. Throughout the 24-hours without technology I felt isolated and out of touch with the outside world, as if I was missing out on some important occurrence that everyone but me knew of. It never occurred to me how dependent I am on technology. Everything from entertainment to my means of communication revolves around technology, which is not difficult to believe in this day and age."* - **Amanda**

This fall, I assigned a unique (and not particularly welcomed) experience to the 19 students in my First-Year Seminar, a transition-to-college course for first-year students. Following an example set by Professor Danna Walker in an experiment she employed with her "Understanding Mass Media" class at American University in Washington D.C., I too wanted to answer the question "[c]ould a class of college students survive without iPods, cellphones, computers and TV from one sunrise to the next?"[43] So I too had my class try to maintain a 24-hour "technology fast" and then write an essay about it. I wasn't particularly surprised by their experience and the difficulty of this experiment; I was, however, quite impressed by some of their powerful reflections. Many felt quite disconnected from everything as a result of this experience, and found the whole experiment to be very challenging.

*"What made it harder for me wasn't the fact that I wasn't using media; it was the fact that I had it and I couldn't use it."* - **Maria**

Several found the experience to be enlightening, realizing that they could "survive" without their cellphones for 24 hours, as difficult as it might be. They came to new conclusions – some different from others – about technology's place in their world.

---

[43] Danna L. Walker, "The Longest Day," *Washington Post*, August 5, 2007.

*"This was a great experience; I learned that I could handle not using my electronic devices for an entire day. It was tough because I couldn't talk with my friends all the time, and take care of a few minor things. However I did manage. . . . Technology makes things easier for people in their lives, but it is not necessary in order to be happy or successful; it is just the cherry on top."* - **Adam**

*"If anyone believes technology does not rule their life they are wrong. I attempted to make it twenty-four hours without technology and I failed horribly. I realized that every day my life revolves around technology. I use my computer about a billion times a day and I use my phone more than twenty times a day."* - **Greg**

A few of my students determined a distinct difference in the quality and content of their communications, now interacting with people face-to-face versus through their all too typical IM or text messages.

*"By actually looking for my friends whenever I needed to talk to them rather than calling them, I noticed the radical differences between communicating through technology instead of approaching someone. The conversation becomes more efficient because you can say everything you wish without sending multiple messages and without getting distracted. You can see the expressions of the person through their gestures, which allows you to notice many things that a phone call or messenger chat can't tell you."* - **Gabriela**

*"We ended up playing TOO many games of Monopoly, Go Fish, Crazy Eights, and Guess Who. Now that I look back on it, it was a lot of time that I got to spend actually talking to and having fun with my little sister. . . . During my technology free period, I found that I could focus so much more on what is actually important to me. I could focus on my relationships with my family, stay healthy, and think about what I had to do for school or work. I felt much more level-headed and I felt like I could manage my life better without the distractions of media. Although some media is important, I think I have already realized that I have cut down on my Facebook usage, TV watching, and pointless texting. This 24 hour period was undoubtedly difficult at times, but overall I found it rather worthwhile. It opened my eyes to everything that media covers up."* - **Laura**

Some realized that they weren't quite as busy as they thought. A common refrain among college students is that there is not enough time in the day for all the work that is assigned to them. When they say that they spend more than six hours a day doing homework, I often ask them if they are doing anything else during that same time, such as surfing the web, e-mailing or IM'ing friends, and so forth.

*My first thought when I woke up was to check my mail, go on Facebook and Skype to chat with friends and family. I realized that I couldn't do that, and had absolutely no idea what else to do without using my phone or the internet. The hardest thing to do was reject all the incoming calls on my phone. It seemed so easy to pick up the phone and talk to everyone, so it took a lot of will power to refrain from doing so. It was also extremely tempting to go on Facebook, check my mail and chat on Skype. Without doing those things I realized how much time I actually have on my hands. I figured out that I don't really need a thirty-six hour day to get all my work done because without technology it feels like there really are thirty-six hours in a day." -* **Sharon**

Lots of the students were relieved to end the experiment, though overwhelmed by their re-entry to the digital world.

*"The fact that I had to plan my day around not being able to use technology is a scary thought. The next morning I had 43 new emails, 13 text messages, and five calls that I had missed." -* **Ryan**

*"My life is very much focused around technology. During a normal day there is not a span of more than an hour other than sleeping that I do not have exposure to technology. I always take notes on my computer; I always have to have my phone on and with me." -* **Juan**

Finally, several had some significant epiphanies regarding their, and others', over-reliance on media, and actually vowed to make some changes in their own lives.

*"I have just completed my 24 hours free of media. It's a relief to be on the laptop again. At first I thought that 24 hours would be easy as they usually tend to go by fast. But I reflected throughout the day that the hours go by faster since I am either chatting with friends or getting distracted by nonsense (i.e. Facebook or YouTube). The two biggest wastes of time ever created." -* **Matias**

*"All three of my roommates do not have this assignment to do and therefore are still on their computers. I, as the only one in the room who is neither typing on computer nor texting on cell phone, suddenly felt completely excluded. What strikes me even more is seeing how little that my roommates are communicating with each other. Everyone is living in their own Facebook and AIM group. The modern technology suddenly served as an excuse to not communicate with each other. . . . The next morning, the first thing I do after I open my eyes is to press the power button of my computer. Everything is back to normal. I sadly realize how little control I have over my life outside of media and am even sadder to realize how little I can do to change it. Because it is not something I can fight against by myself as an individual, it requires the awareness of everyone around me. Maybe we should have a global media-free day, and then people will realize how much they've lost." -* **Yue**

*"I had never stopped to realize how much our generation depends on technology until I had been asked not use it for 24 hours. These were the longest 24 hours of my life. Everything in my life is centered around technology like my cellphone, texting, Facebook, and instant messenger. I had to occupy myself with other things that I was not quite so used to. It was weird not being able to open my laptop first thing in the morning or check my messages before going out. I don't know how my parents did it. Back when they were growing up no one had cellphones, and computers were not a way of communicating. Everything was a lot more personal and you would actually enjoy people's company. That's the only downside I have learned in today's society. Kids and teens don't appreciate what is given to us. They rely on technology to communicate with others and less on public discourse. . . . Technology has rapidly grown over the years and it's just a part of our generation's lifestyle. . . . However, I have learned a lesson from doing this. I learned that it means so much more to me spending time with people in person than it does communicating through technology. It allowed me to be more sociable and willing to take on new activities and get my work done. When I shut off technology for just a segment of my day I think it'll be more helpful in the long run. It doesn't have to be for 24 hours, but maybe just a chunk of my day I will cut out technology from my everyday lifestyle. I will interact with more people and try new things. This was very useful and I'm going to start to implement it more and hopefully it'll help me in the future!"* - **Morgan**

It is amazing and telling to me that these very powerful reactions came from one day without their usual access to technology – not a week, not a month, but a single day. And from it, these students have very perceptively summed up what many researchers, including myself, have found to be unintended consequences of the digital revolution. *Born Digital: Understanding the First Generation of Digital Natives* describes the impact of technology on today's younger generations: "[m]ajor aspects of their lives – social interactions, friendships, civic activities – are mediated by digital technologies. ... Most notable, however, is the way the digital era has transformed how people live their lives and relate to one another and the world around them."[44]

I am in much agreement with the authors. Technology has had tremendous impact on the generation that grew up with it – both positive and negative. Strauss and Howe expressed concern that the Millennial generation would struggle with creative tasks, most likely due to the constant exposure to stimuli that keep them from flexing that creative muscle with enough frequency. In discussing the implications of Millennials' lifelong teamwork experiences for the college classroom, Strauss and Howe suggest that "[g]etting Millennials to apply themselves over a sustained period

---

[44] John Palfrey and Urs Gasser, *Born Digital: Understanding the First Generation of Digital Natives* (New York: Basic Books, 2008).

of time to an independent or creative task will require careful thought and classroom planning."[45] Is this true? Has their concern played out? If so, the implications are unlikely to end with college, and will certainly manifest extensively in their work lives. Dorothy and Jerome Singer raise this fascinating question in *Imagination and Play in the Electronic Age*: "[h]ave the new electronic media introduced changes in the attention capacities of children and adults and in the style and structure of their consciousness and imagination?"[46] I would assert that a lifetime of "noise" filling their every waking moment has had an adverse effect on the development of that creative muscle. While this noise is not just a stream of media through the TV, computer, cell phone, I-Pod, etc., (I maintain that the very hyper-scheduling of the Millennial youth – with school, followed by soccer, followed by violin lessons, followed by tutoring, and on and on – is part of this noise as well), media is a big part of this problem. There...I said it: problem.

Singer and Singer state, "[t]elevision was now an important environmental feature in a child's life and one that surely must be taken into consideration as a contributor to a child's development, especially to a child's capacity for imagination."[47] They discuss that children often create imaginative games based on what they view on TV. The Singers lament that there isn't a lot of research out there that discusses in a similar way the impact of other electronic media, such as the internet on children's development, but I recognize that as more and more time is spent interfacing with TV and these other forms of media, less and less time is spent doing traditionally creative activities, or engaging in imaginative thought or play. Though there are some notions that challenge how we view creativity – thus my choice of the term "traditionally creative activities" – and I will get to that. With less time spent being creative, our kids have grown up with less developed creative skills, and that has turned them into less creative young adults.

---

[45] Neil Howe and William Strauss, *Millennials Go to College*, (LifeCourse Associates, 2003).

[46] Dorothy G. and Jerome L. Singer, *Imagination and Play in the Electronic Age* (Massachusetts: Harvard University Press, 2005).

[47] Ibid.

*"That lid on the shoebox that is the current generation shelters in broader and more abstract ways. Not that there is a lack of creativity or intelligence, just that I think it's harder to think out-side of the box, in part because the box is so big. Don't get me wrong, this can also be a good thing. More influences can be gathered, perspective can come faster, schools and other posi-tive institutions can be trusted, and journeys can start with a far more filled backpack than before. But more toys don't necessar-ily teach more lessons, and more information does not especially foster critical thinking. But perhaps this generation is less about a specific statement [and more about] one that stops and sorts out the tools we've accumulated, i.e., the internet, and how it creates, effects, nourishes, and undermines the hive."*
Roger F. Prahl, Lawyer, Litigation Services

To further this issue, Millennials read less. A November, 2007 report from the National Endowment for the Arts describes a significant decline in reading in the United States. The study reports that the typical 15- to 24-year-old watches two hours of television a day, and spends only about seven minutes a day reading for leisure. About a third of 13-year-olds read daily, and the percentage of non-readers has more than doubled since 1984, from 9 percent to 19 percent in 2004.[48] Singer and Singer discuss the important creative development that occurs with reading: "[W}hen we read, a more complicated process occurs than when we view television. We are engaged in the active process of encoding the words on the printed page by combining discrete letters. From strings of words, thoughts are generated, associations are made, and images are constructed."[49] Lest we question this relevance to us as employers, we should take note of the conclusions of the NEA: "[n]early two-thirds of employers ranked reading comprehension 'very important' for high school graduates. Yet 38 percent consider most high school graduates deficient in this basic skill."[50]

---

[48] National Endowment for the Arts News Room, "National Endowment for the Arts Announces New Reading Study," November 19, 2007, 12/14/08 [http://www.nea.gov/news/news07/TRNR.html].

[49] Dorothy G. and Jerome L. Singer, *Imagination and Play in the Electronic Age* (Massachusetts: Harvard University Press, 2005).

[50] National Endowment for the Arts News Room, "National Endowment for the Arts Announces New Reading Study," November 19, 2007, 12/14/08 [http://www.nea.gov/news/news07/TRNR.html].

It may be time that we view creativity through a new lens. As a Gen X-er, I have defined creativity by pretty strict standards for the overwhelming majority of my life, and am only recently shifting my paradigm just a bit on this one. I still maintain that Millennials' artistic and imaginative forces have really been hindered by the influences discussed in this chapter, but there are many ways in which they are more creative (or at least more *DIFFERENTLY* creative) than the generations that preceded them. Look at YouTube, which is just one example of this – but there are so many others: blogging, Wikipedia, their Facebook sites, and so forth. I believe that the primary users of YouTube are teens and young adults. Certainly companies are realizing that YouTube is a great way to reach a potential consumer base. There is some really creative stuff out there on YouTube! There's also a lot of junk, but that doesn't discount the innovation amidst it. Millennials are using digital cameras, cell phones, and video cameras to create their own short movies and other forms of self-expression to post to the web. I had friends who tried their hand at such artistic endeavors in their teens or early twenties, but I could count them on one hand, or even a couple of fingers. Technology has not only enabled, but really inspired, a whole new art form. We just have to learn to see it that way. "The Internet has unleashed an explosion of creativity – and along with it thousands of new forms of creative expression – on a vast scale. These new forms of expression are unlike anything the world has ever seen before. Digital Natives are increasingly engaged in creating information, knowledge, and entertainment in online environments."[51] There are so many avenues available now for this form of public expression.

> *"Technology is typically a positive influence with LanguageCorps participants. It allows them to stay in touch with friends and family while overseas, research their new environment, and write about their experiences. Many participants write lengthy blogs about their daily life abroad, and several have been published by travel or international magazines."*
> *Jan Patton*
> *Admissions Director*
> *LanguageCorps*

The development of these creative technological skills has great payoff in the workplace. All of this playing with computers has really developed

---

[51] John Palfrey and Urs Gasser, Born Digital: *Understanding the First Generation of Digital Natives* (New York: Basic Books, 2008).

those skill sets to a tremendous level. When I was in high school, I took a computer class and learned some of the earlier home computer user programming languages, but I did not grow up working and experimenting on a personal computer. Millennials did, and they are exceptionally comfortable continuing to play, figuring things out, designing new programs or websites, and using online communities to enhance the work environment. Companies revel in the efficiencies that Millennials can help to bring to the workplace through the creative employment of technology.

> *"Positives: they learn new technologies quickly, they are more adaptable to change and they use technology in creative ways."*
> Sarah Olson, Director of Recruiting, Berry, Dunn, McNeil & Parker, CPA
>
> *"The positives are many – they are able to quickly gather and conduct research, they are better able to pull together graphically rich presentations, they are comfortable multi-tasking. Through use of technologies they have been able to reduce project timelines."*
> Irene DeNigris
> Director, Global University Recruitment
> Johnson & Johnson

There are concerns, however, that these efficiencies come with great cost. I have long maintained that the Millennial Generation really struggles with exhibiting patience and sitting with uncertainty. As I have discussed, as great multi-taskers, Millennials are busy at all times, and technology is a major tool for them as they try to keep up with it all. A colleague recently told me a story of getting a call from a student regarding some academic advising questions. When she remarked that the connection wasn't great and seemed kind of "windy," he told her that he was calling her from the ski slopes, where he was snowboarding! I certainly do my own share of multi-tasking with occasional calls from my cell phone in the car, but I don't think it would ever occur to me, or many of my Generation X or Boomer colleagues, to take care of business from the slopes! But this does raise the obvious question of the efficacy of multi-tasking. "'The human brain literally cannot do two things at once,' says Sandra Bond Chapman, Ph.D., chief director of the University of Texas at Dallas Center for Brain Health. 'It quickly toggles back and forth from one task to the other, taking its toll on our efficiency,' she notes."[52]

---

[52] Charlotte Latvala, "De-Stress Your Weeknights," *Good Housekeeping Magazine*, January 2009.

> *"They try to do everything by email, Skype, instant messaging, etc. It is very hard to get them to "meet" to discuss or call to discuss. Their answers are like email or IM answers: short and not very revealing.*
>
> *They do have speed and knowledge and no fear of technology, but they seem to use it for fun and not necessarily for work. They want answers so fast, they don't like to work or research to find answers."*
> Susan Shaer, Executive Director, WAND
> (Women's Action for New Directions)

Unfortunately, this lifelong experience with the immediacy of technology may also cause them to struggle with uncertainty and thus need immediate gratification. On more than one occasion I've come in at 8 a.m. to an e-mail sent by a student at 7 a.m. that asks why I haven't replied yet... and it refers to the original e-mail sent to me at 2:30 a.m. They have been conditioned by the propinquity that they have experienced throughout their whole lives, much of it enabled by technology.

Think about it this way: when I was a kid and needed to reach a parent at home, I would call and let the phone ring...and ring...and ring. Our little family rule was that if no one picked up by ten rings, then we should try again later. Now, when young people, or any of us, really, try to reach someone, what do we do if we can't we reach them at home? We call their cell phones. Or maybe we even skip trying them at home and just go right to the cell. And if they don't pick up, do we leave a message? No, of course not, because "they will see that I called." We do not even expend the time, energy, or patience to leave a quick message.

I am not indicting Millennials here; I think we all do this – it has become our habituation. The difference here is that Millennials grew up with it. They grew up always being able to reach someone quite quickly, if not immediately, at the other end of their cellphone. They grew up with the immediacy of e-mail. In fact, we are seeing that e-mail may "take too long" for today's youth. As Chad Lorenz discusses in "The Death of E-mail" for *Slate Magazine Online*, "[e]veryone was especially eager to send messages to my niece, a kid who wasn't all that chatty on the phone but was almost always glued to her PC. But while the rest of us happily exchanged forwards and life updates, she almost never piped up. Eventually, I sussed out the truth: She was too busy sending IMs and text messages to bother with e-mail. That's when I realized that my agility with e-mail no longer marked me as a tech-savvy young adult. It made me a lame old fogey."[53] Lorenz cites a July 2005 Pew Research Center report on "Family, Friends, and Community," which discusses that while e-mail has been the most popular application on the internet for many years, it may be beginning its decline as a result of teens, predilection for instant messaging and similar technologies. "The presence of email in teens' lives has persisted, and the number that use email continues to surpass those who use IM. However, when asked about which modes of communication they use most often when communicating with friends, online teens consistently choose IM over email in a wide array of contexts. Teens who participated in focus groups for this study said that they view email as something you use to talk to 'old people,' institutions, or to send complex instructions to large groups. When it comes to casual written conversation, particularly when talking with friends, online instant messaging is the clearly the mode of choice for today's online teens."[54] This to me underscores the immediacy issue; Millennial teens are finding and utilizing faster mechanisms for communication, ones that do not require them to wait even a moment for the answer to their question, the exchange of a greeting with a friend, or the gathering of "data" on what others are up to – through their posting of "away messages" that provide detailed information on their comings and goings. And today's Millennial teens are tomorrow's adult employees, taught by these experiences.

*"It hurts. Gen Y just wants to get things done. There is always a sense of immediacy. There's a lot of impatience. Gen Y is full of productivity machines. We get things done, we figure out how to use technology to complete an assignment as fast as we can. Positives and negatives for both. Opportunity to try new things because we can complete them so quickly. First time in history that the younger generation knows more about the newest technology than the older generation."* (cont. on page 73)

---

[53] Chad Lorenz, "The Death of E-Mail: Teenagers are abandoning their Yahoo! and Hotmail accounts. Do the rest of us have to?" *Slate Magazine Online*, November 14, 2007, 12/16/08 [http://www.slate.com/id/2177969/pagenum/all/].

[54] Amanda Lenhart, Mary Madden, and Paul Hitlin, "Teens and Technology," July 27, 2005, Pew Internet & American Life Project.

*(cont. from page 72)*
*"In the past with new technologies (driving a car, etc.), it was always the older people teaching the young people how to use technology and now it's different."*
Ryan Healy (Millennial)
Co-Founder, Brazen Careerist

The consequences of this immediacy can play out in many ways. It can be argued that Millennials are impatient about a lot of things. They don't always spend the time needed to get the job "done right" because they want to get on to the next thing.

*"There is some problem with the expectation of immediacy (again - youth generally?) E.g. the Wiki/blog curse = Wikipedia vs. reading a book on the subject. Who needs context when you can have 'facts' and figures? Reacting quickly to information is also tricky. Although more aware than others about the foibles of the quality of the information on the internet, they are quick to promulgate it once convinced. So if a blogger can convince you...."*
Roger F. Prahl, Lawyer, Litigation Services

*"Millennials rely on technology to manage routine. I doubt any in this age group manually balances their check books. Sometimes they rely on technology too much. Formal communications might appear to be written in haste because the [M]illennial did not take time to proof read their text or data."*
Seth Nable, Manager Training and Development
Human Resources OnProcess Technology

They are also impatient with their own career advancement. This is tied to a lot of things, in my opinion, including the messaging they have received through constant celebration and accolades about all the success that is due to them, but I argue that this immediacy factor plays a large part in it as well. I recently spoke to a group of Millennials at one company, sharing some research findings about them, and they honed right in on the issue of expectation of immediate advancement and reward. Just as one of them expressed frustration of the company's lack of recognition that she had already "paid her dues" at the company (having interned there during her college years), another asked if their personal experience of impatience with waiting for promotions and other recognition is tied to this overall generational psychography. How do I answer this? I genuinely told her that of course I can't say for sure that her personal feelings come from just being a Millennial, but it certainly is consistent with research findings.

*"I do think the immediacy thing has a negative effect in some cases, as immediate results are not always possible when it comes to change, career progression, compensation, etc."*
Anonymous
HR Business Partner, Multimedia Publishing Company

*"Negatives [include] an unwillingness to "pay your dues" before you start running the organization."*
Sarah Olson
Director of Recruiting
Berry, Dunn, McNeil & Parker, CPA

There are so many ways in which Millennials' experience of technology has helped to form them. For quite some time now, I have been talking with audiences about some interesting data I found in "The Internet and Education: Findings of the Pew Internet & American Life Project (2001)." This may seem outdated about seven years later, but actually I think it is even more relevant; this report discusses technology use among youth ages 12-17 in 2001. These youth are today's young adults, our new Millennial employees! And their use of technology has played a part in how they interface in the world. It has informed what they expect from others, including their employers.

*"Technology is amazing, but I totally agree that a dependence on it can have a negative consequence and that it brings many distractions. In terms of communication, Millennials again want instant gratification. 'Where are you right now?' Or 'what is the answer now?' Text messaging, high speed internet and emails allow them to communicate so quickly that they never have to learn to be patient or learn how to deal with confrontation face to face. This type of communication is efficient but not necessarily effective."* (cont. on page 75)

*(cont. from page 74)*

*"We've seen in our office that important messages can be distorted or lose their value if they are not communicated face to face. Also, when you are receiving three messages at once from three different people, it's very hard to stay focused. Again, information overload. This generation is easily distracted.*

*Communication is something we continue to work on in our office. We haven't found the perfect solution yet but we are working towards it."*
Becky Girola
Director of Recruiting, Northwestern Mutual Financial Network

I fully believe that the Millennial Generation has been defined by its technology. And that technology has been all but omnipresent. In 2001, 73 percent of youth 12-17 (that's 17 million youth) in the United States were online and, wow, were they active:

- 21% of online youth had four or more e-mail addresses;

- 92% of online teens used e-mail;

- 74% of online teens used IM;

- 84% of teens owned at least one personal media device and 44% owned two or more;

- 85% of students at supported colleges used Facebook;

- 71% of online teens said that they used the Internet as the major source for most recent big school project;

- The average teen spent 7.8 hours per week talking to friends through technology;

- 75% of online teens — or about two-thirds of all teenagers — were using instant messaging;

- 48% of teens who were using instant messaging said they exchange IMs at least once every day; and

- One in five teens said IM is **the main way** they communicate with friends.[55]

As I said, as of this writing in early 2009, this data is pushing ten years old (and, not surprisingly, several more recent Pew reports discuss an substantial increase in this usage amongst today's youth – I warn you now, this issue may only be amplified in the future), but it remains relevant given its impact on the psychography of these now adult Millennial workers. Let's look back at a few fascinating quotes from young people interviewed for the Pew Report.

*"I multi-task every single second I am online. At this very moment, I am watching TV, checking my email every two minutes, reading a newsgroup about who shot JFK, burning some music to a CD and writing this message."* - **17-year-old boy**

*"I do so many things at once. I'm always talking to people through instant messenger and then I'll be checking email or doing homework or playing games AND talking on the phone at the same time."* - **15-year-old girl**

*"I get bored if it's not all going at once, because everything has gaps – waiting for an IM, waiting for a website to come up, commercials on TV, etc."* - **17-year-old girl** [56]

These are your Millennial employees. That 17-year-old girl is now your 26-year-old employee, and she has been conditioned by technology to become bored and frustrated during the momentary gap as she waits for a response to an e-mail or for her web browser to open. This is concerning to me, and I think it has significant consequences for her, and similar Millennials', experience in the workplace.

---

[55] Amanda Lenhart, Maya Simon, and Mike Graziano, "The Internet and Education: Findings of the Pew Internet & American Life Project," September 1, 2001, Pew Internet & American Life Project.

[56] Ibid.

> *"Millennials have extremely short attention spans and are attempting to multitask. Rather than completing one project very well, they are touching several projects that do not get the attention they deserve, resulting in just meeting or falling short of the goal."*
> Cynthia Levinson
> On-Site Supervisor at State Street Corporation, Kelly Complete

This theme of impatience is not the only consequence that we see with the dramatic use of e-mail and IM for communication. Educators have been long-lamenting what they see as a serious decline in analytical skills ability with today's youth, and blame these technologies for being somewhat responsible for the issues. Nicholas Carr, in his recent attention-grabbing article "Is Google Making Us Stupid?", talks about his own experience with declining attention span: "Over the past few years I've had an uncomfortable sense that someone, or something, has been tinkering with my brain, remapping the neural circuitry, reprogramming the memory. My mind isn't going — so far as I can tell — but it's changing. I'm not thinking the way I used to think. I can feel it most strongly when I'm reading. Immersing myself in a book or a lengthy article used to be easy. My mind would get caught up in the narrative or the turns of the argument, and I'd spend hours strolling through long stretches of prose. That's rarely the case anymore. Now my concentration often starts to drift after two or three pages. I get fidgety, lose the thread, begin looking for something else to do. I feel as if I'm always dragging my wayward brain back to the text. The deep reading that used to come naturally has become a struggle." And, he maintains, many of his also quite literate and literary friends attribute this to the superficiality of time spent surfing the web. While he does acknowledge that we do not as yet have data from long-term neurological and psychological experiments on this issue, there are experiments that have shown just how shallow and cursory most of our web reading is. And his brain, like mine, was not formed in the looming shadow of this kind of influence. If Google is making Gen X-ers and Boomers "stupid," what has it done for the minds of Millennials, weaned on the internet?

We should pause for a moment to acknowledge that it is not just the Millennials using these forms of technology; it is "trickling up," at least partially due to their influence, on those of us who are older. It's not just the impact that Carr discusses, but in many other areas as well. Writing about Facebook, Neil Swidey discusses it growing appeal to the over-

35 crowd: "[I]t's been only two years since it opened its gates to those outside the college crowd. Today, people ages 35 to 54 represent about one-fifth of the site's 120 million users, and in the last year, that segment grew nearly six times as fast as the 13-to-34 group."[57] Obviously, that growth had been in large part due to the site being opened to those without an ".edu" address, but it is more than that. This is a place where Millennials' influence has been extraordinarily strong, and continues to be. A recent press release from Sprint indicates that while those who are 30 and younger obviously continue to be the most hearty group of texters, they are pushing their parents to text as well. The number of adults who are texting has risen from a couple of years ago when, according to a 2006 Pew Research study, 13 percent of adults aged 50-64 used the text function on their cellphone. This recent Sprint study informs us that 20 percent of adults aged 55 to 64 now send text messages. And it's all because of the kids: 76 percent of adults in this age group who are texting are sending the messages to their kids.[58] The press release goes on to discuss just why texting has taken off among the older crowd: "[w]ith [their] kids away at college or living in different cities, texting is a fast and efficient way for parents to stay in touch. According to a survey conducted by Opinion Research Corp. (ORC), a text is far more likely to elicit a quick response than voice mail. In fact, those under the age of 30 are four times more likely to respond within minutes to a text message compared to a voice mail, and 91 percent respond to a text message within one hour. Adults 30 and older are also quick to text – and are twice as likely to respond within minutes to a text message as compared to a voice message."[59] And there has begun to be a workplace expectation of adaptation to these new technologies, regardless of where you fall in the generational spectrum, as Dan Kadlec writes in "How Not to Act Your Age at Work" for *Money* magazine. "If you don't know how to integrate these latest communication technologies into your workday – or worse, you resist them altogether – you run the risk of appearing old and hopelessly out of touch. That isn't good anytime, but it's especially perilous in a weak economy when, as a mature worker with

---

[57] Neil Swidey, "Friends in a Facebook World," *Boston Globe Magazine*, November 30, 2008.

[58] Opinion Research Corporation (Press Release), "Thanks to Millennials, Older Adults Increasingly Adopt Text Messaging," October 22, 2008 [http://www.marketwatch.com/news/story/thanks-millennials -older-adults-increasingly/story.aspx?guid=%7BC884966A- EFAD-424B-8D22-2488C13D9680%7D&dist=hppr].

[59] Ibid.

a relatively big salary, you're most vulnerable to cutbacks."[60] The very fact that there is a need for such advice as "four tech skills that folks under 35 know almost intuitively..." in order to "be seen as vital and youthful (in spirit if not in years)"[61] says a great deal about the influence of the younger generation on the older in this matter.

There are obvious benefits for enabling strong business ties – as well as family and other social ones –, but all of this does come with some consequences. If we think that the web is having its impact on how we think and comprehend, we just have to ask any educator – at any level – how e-mail, texting, and IM'ing is impacting the writing skills of their students. This is where the rubber is really hitting the road on this one. And it isn't getting better as these Millennials get to the work environment. Years of bad habits are ingrained, and employers are getting pretty frustrated.

*"Negative aspects of the exposure to technology come in the form of communication. I find [M]illennials will send an email before picking up the phone to call someone. There is also a concern for written communication. Email communication will sometimes contain 'text messaging' language that is not appropriate within all business cultures. This different mode of communication can easily create barriers for success between generations."*
Matt Duren
College Recruiting Manager, GEICO

*"Technology pervades every aspect of their lives. This extends to the workplace in obvious ways and in less obvious ways. They are more comfortable using productivity software, which is helpful. However, they also spend a lot of time on the internet, YouTube and networking sites while at work. They don't turn off their cell phones or distinguish between personal and professional. They also share a lot more private information on Facebook and via email. This reduces productivity and puts our organization at risk."*
Anonymous
Assistant Director
Career Development Non-Profit Organization

---

[60] Dan Kadlec, "How Not to Act Your Age at Work," *Money*, December 2008.

[61] Ibid.

The issue is not just about their communication skills, or where they are lacking, but where and how Millennials feel most comfortable communicating. Remember, as per the Pew Report, 75 percent of online teens in 2001 were using instant messaging, with 48 percent saying they were using it at least once every day, and one in five teens reporting that IM is the main way that they communicate with friends. These are some pretty serious habits; they have come to believe that this is a perfectly reasonable way to interact with anyone on any matter. And maybe it is. But this represents a significant shift for the way business is done at most organizations, and not all are on board with it. Older professionals have spent their careers talking to clients, customers, and colleagues in person or on the phone, and while they see a lot of benefit to the tech-orientation of these new employees, many see this shift in communication trends as difficult, or even unacceptable.

*"I have seen both highly skilled Millennials and low skilled Millennials. There is a cultural gap. Working in non-profit and hiring many ethnically diverse staff, it is evident that there is a technology skills gap. The positive of having staff with proficient technology skills is they think differently about how to communicate - usually it's more efficient, and they do not hesitate to use technology to store, retrieve or illustrate data. They look forward to technological skills trainings and put value in things like the organizations website and technology infrastructure. One of the negatives I see is that the actual skill of communicating to others is not there. Millennials communicate in sound bites, they don't temper their thoughts or feelings and they don't think about the consequences of what they put in email or text. They don't worry about how it's heard, received or understood. And...grammar and spelling are a lost art."*

Sharon Zimmerman
Deputy Director, WAND (Women's Action for New Directions)
(formerly Vice President for Programs and Services, Goodwill Industries)

Perhaps we have a lot to learn from our new Millennial colleagues regarding the utilization of newer technologies to reach and communicate with customers or business partners, but we also need to remind them that, to many of us, these do not represent communication or conversation. For many, a phone call can never be replaced by a text message or an

IM, at least not yet. To get there is likely to be a major cultural shift for Gen X-ers and Boomers, but it also seems that to "leave there" is a major cultural shift for Millennials.

> *"On the negative side - they sometimes are more comfortable communicating through a computer vs. in person. Their communication skills are sometimes not business appropriate - they blur the informal social styles into the workplace."*
> Irene DeNigris
> Director, Global University Recruitment Johnson & Johnson
>
> *"Phone conversations are a lost skill. They prefer to text and email."*
> Ed Ayala
> Vice President, Strategies for Wealth

Appropriateness is a recurring theme with technology and Millennials. It is not just an issue of what mode of communication should be utilized for professional communication, but also what is okay to do at work in general. Perhaps because work and home have been so blurred given how much informal telecommuting people do as a result of the near-constant technological access, it suggests license to use technology to do personal things while at work.

> *"They also seem to have an issue with separation of their time; the technology used at work should be used only for work, not for personal use. Although companies have been using firewall technology for making this more difficult for personnel to do, often you will see these employees using personal devices on company time."*
> Cynthia Levinson
> On-Site Supervisor at State Street Corporation, Kelly Complete

This clearly poses difficulties for managers and colleagues alike who characterize this as lacking in work ethic; I am not sure that is an accurate representation – because I think it is fairly clear that Millennials are not actually lazy in the workplace, but they do have a different way of looking at the blend of work and play.

Perhaps one of the most concerning aspects to all of this, for me, is the apparent inability to "sit in silence" for the Millennials. I recently spoke to a large audience that was probably about 50 percent Boomers, 40 percent X-ers, and maybe 10 percent Millennials. At one point, a Boomer in the audience wanted to know if this generation ever just sits and thinks; do they ever take time to just reflect on their life or their day? Rather than answer the question myself, I asked the Millennials to respond themselves. It took about four different articulations of the same question for one young woman to understand what was being asked. First she talked about how her web browser is programmed to automatically go to CNN.com so that she is tuned in to what is going on in the world, and then she discussed how she and her friends do discuss the world happenings. Finally, when she was essentially confronted with the very concrete question of "do you ever just do nothing," she had to admit that she doesn't. And, even worse, she says that all of her friends are just like her.

On November 26, 2008, National Public Radio's *On Point with Tom Ashbrook* did a show on "Digital Youth." On Point's website describes the program: "[t]he Internet is producing the most socially plugged in, caught up, networked and aware generation since — what? Maybe the *Mayflower*. Parents worry about all that time online. A big new study says, 'chill.' The kids are OK."[62] Several guests and callers weighed in on the recently completed three-year study of teens and the Internet by Mizuko Ito, a research scientist at the University of California, Irvine. What bothered me most was that no one, not even Tom Ashbrook himself, asked the question, "what about downtime?" One consequence of being constantly tapped into to media is that one is **always** hooked in, never just sitting and reflecting. I could ask any psychologist or child development specialist if taking time to reflect on one's day is important for personal development and the ability to develop key life skills like coping and resiliency, and they would resoundingly argue that it is beyond important, and is in fact imperative. Millennials are the first to tell us, and I have heard it many times, that they really do not allow themselves this time or activity. They are too busy rushing from one thing to the next, and when they are not rushing, they are filling their lives and thoughts with all that technology has to offer. They not only come to the workplace with some underdeveloped critical life skills as a result, they are also quite unpracticed at taking time to think and process, arguably essential skills for an effective employee.

---

[62] *On Point with Tom Ashbrook*, "Digital Youth," November 26, 2008, 12/21/08 [http://www.onpointradio.org/shows/2008/11/digital-youth/].

*"I have found in the last two organizations I worked for that Millennials bring a lot of professional immaturity to the workplace. They bring their personal dramas and create workplace dramas. They do not understand professional boundaries and do not hesitate to mix business and pleasure. Workplace protocols, etiquette and even policies seem to have no bearing on how Millennials behave sometimes. Goodwill did put formal coaching programs in place to help with these issues. Monthly lunches with the VP of HR were set up to provide a place to discuss these issues. At WAND (my current place of employment) the Executive Director has asked me to work with staff one on one on some of these issues, using coaching as a way to provide support."*

Sharon Zimmerman
Deputy Director, WAND (Women's Action for New Directions)
(formerly Vice President for Programs and Services, Goodwill Industries)

"'Quiet reflective time" was the phrase the speaker used to describe what he needed to do his work most effectively. So valuable was this time that he blocked out days at a time on his schedule months in advance. The speaker was none other than Jim Collins, author of *Good to Great*. Collins explains that he might have meetings during these reflective days, but he purposely kept his schedule loose so he would have time to think, research and write. John Maxwell writes about making time for thinking and reflecting in his book, *Thinking for a Change*, in which he advises creating physical space, a chair, a room, a garden, someplace where you can go and gain perspective on the topic. Such advice is not reserved strictly for management gurus. The late Skip LeFauve, president of Saturn Corporation and high-ranking executive at General Motors, advised busy people to schedule time for reflection on their calendars, much like Collins does."[63]

These are important concepts, but ones that are completely antithetical to Millennials' experience and conditioning. So how can organizations help to foster growth in this area, and react overall to the massive impact that technology plays in the way Millennials approach life and work? If we (loosely) apply Newton's Third Law of Motion, "for every action, there is an equal and opposite reaction," **how do we react?**

---

[63] John Baldoni, "Putting Reflection into Gear," 12/27/08 [http://articles.directorym.com/Putting_Reflection_into_Gear-a854622.html].

- ## Add to existing leadership development programs.

Many companies, particularly larger corporations, have substantial leadership or management training programs. These have been around for decades, but smaller companies are now beginning to see more and more the wisdom of these kinds of programs, even if they aren't as robust as the ones at major worldwide companies.

*"I am the training manager of a small company, 500 employees in the Metro West [Boston] area. Two years ago, we embarked on a strategy to recruit this group of workers straight from college, give them serious responsibilities and see what they can do. The results have been very positive across the board, senior executives clamor for these employees on their teams. In order to facilitate their transition to the world of work, we instituted a Leadership Training Program. Monthly, the group of ten employees meets with either senior internal leaders, or outside professionals (including an executive coach, which they love). I facilitate the group and as a result have gotten to know these individuals pretty well. I believe that Millennials have a very egalitarian view on work, respect knowledge, are goal driven, and need reminders of the value and importance of their work."*
Seth Nable, Manager Training and Development
Human Resources OnProcess Technology

But what isn't being directly addressed in these programs are some topics that older employees, the ones who direct these "curriculums," may take for granted as obvious principles that needn't be taught. The new generation of employees may actually need to be educated on issues of workplace etiquette, for lack of better terminology. Everything from what is appropriate to post on your Facebook page to what is okay to do with your work computer. Millennials are extraordinarily accustomed to the use of social networking sites to establish and maintain connections. New college roommates don't initially connect via the phone anymore; they "friend" each other on Facebook. Many colleges have learned to embrace this instead of fighting it. In the past, colleges have employed a wide variety of mechanisms, including technological, to try to connect students and help them to form a sense of unity, but now they realize how Facebook and similar sites can be a boon for this effort. And they can be for business organizations as well, in the effort to forge these connections with and amidst their employees.

However, social media sites can cause us to blur the lines between work and personal, and this can get into some dangerous territory. *Wired Magazine* recently described the new jargon of "frolleague: n. a work colleague friended on a social networking site and thus granted access to personal information, from blog entries to stag party pics, that may be perceived as less than professional—or even (if the frolleague happens to be a frupervisor) grounds for dismissal."[64] Millennials, more than anyone, need education around the hazards of "frolleague-ing." This is a generation that has been conditioned, in deep and profound ways, to conduct themselves in ways that are truly foreign to those of us who are older.

> *"As an amusing sidebar, I recently attended a [college alumni] class day event where us alums could sit in on undergraduate courses. I chose a class, and I sat in the back of the room to be unobtrusive. After the lecture had gone on for some time, I looked up from the notes I was taking and glanced at the laptop screens across the room. I saw students posting on Facebook. I saw students instant messaging. I even saw one student writing a cover letter. But I did not see a single student with typed notes of the lecture on his screen. Given that I've recently been to the optometrist and can therefore see a good distance ... well, that's a LOT of students."*
>
> R. Kyle Jones
> President, EduSophia

This is not news to educators; my friend Tobe, who teaches high school science, regularly tells me of "busting" students as they try to text friends with their cellphones, hiding their hands under their desks. This is the next generation of "passing notes" in class, and they have been doing it since they got their cells. The habits persisted through high school and college, and they may be bringing them to the workplace.

Managers are already working on these issues with their young employees, but they are finding themselves repeating company "rules" over and over, often to no avail. It may be time to address these issues in a concrete programmatic way. Millennials need to be actively taught to adapt to new standards of behavior and to their new professional settings, and corpo-

---

[64] Jonathon Keats, "Jargon Watch: Sound Blast, Frolleague, Twiller," *Wired Magazine*, 11/24/08.

rate seminars on workplace behavior – as absurd as it may sound – may be among the most effective tools for re-educating new employees.

> *"Also, while for the most part the individuals were intelligent and hard-working, they spent a huge amount of time and resources IMing, Facebooking, and iTuning. Despite the fact that policies at the firms I have worked at forbid the plugging-in, downloading or installing of personal software, this was done by, I would say, everyone. There were employees who requested CD burners for ostensibly work-related purposes that turned out to be used for personal CD burning. The Millennials seemed to be able to justify anything that would make the workday seem more like a day at home with friends."*
>
> Anonymous
> Manager of paralegals, various New York law firms

Another topic to be addressed in these work-based educational programs is proper business communication. As I discussed earlier in this chapter, there is a great deal of concern among educators about the writing skills of the students of the past decade, and this concern is shared by their employers. "Al Barron, director of career services at Southern University, says most universities are dealing with communication issues. 'It's not just Southern, LSU or Louisiana schools,' he says. 'It's a nationwide problem.' Students, he says, write like they text message, with their own language and rules for spelling and grammar. 'They haven't been able to move in between the two.' Both Southern and LSU have responded to the need to improve communication skills with workshops, presentations and courses."[65] Mr. Barron is not wrong in his assertion that the issue is not limited to his college; these concerns are shared by probably every college around the country. Further, the steps that Southern University and Louisiana State University are taking in combating students' writing deficiencies are not unique either. But despite the fact that all of these measures are being undertaken, Millennials are still rather poor written communicators, and companies have no choice but to deal with it with their new employees. Fair or not, workplace workshops on written communication may be money well spent for an organization trying to build talent and professionalism in their new employees.

---

[65] Marissa Frayer, "From Classroom to Cubicle,"
*The Greater Baton Rouge Business Report,* May 22, 2007.

Finally, perhaps through programs like these, we may even be able to teach what educators and parents have not been able to achieve thus far – how to be reflective. As with many things, the habituation of constant busy-ness with no time for reflection has been strong, and Millennials need to establish some new habits. An effective management training program might be able to foster an appreciation for – at least professionally – the benefit of deliberation, as well as teach a bit about how to do it, if only on work-related issues.

*"We currently have a program called the HIPP (Health Insurance Professional Program) which is a leadership development program. Our current program participants are undergraduate and graduate students that have been identified as high-potential leaders with a strong interest in making a difference in healthcare through the insurance industry. Our current HIPP associates created their own internal website to blog, network, and discuss matters of relevance to them. In this way they are able to be a cohesive group even though they are scattered all over the country."*
Helen Hong
College Relations Manager, WellPoint Inc.

- **Invest in the technology.**

There is much more that companies can and should do in this age of the Millennial beyond working to adapt the new employee to the environment; the fact is, there is a lot of adaptation that the environment needs to do as well. "Millennial generation students and employees (those aged 14 to 27) expect to use their own technology and mobile devices for work and are increasingly choosing their place of employment based on how accommodating companies are to their personal technology preferences."[66] The report goes on to discuss that these employees will insist on state-of-the-art technology, and that more than half the Millennials surveyed made it clear that state-of-the-art technology is an important consideration in selecting where to work.[67]

---

[66] Accenture (Press Release), "'New-Generation Workers' Want Technology Their Way, Accenture Survey Finds," November 5, 2008 [http://newsroom.accenture.com/article_display.cfm?article_id=4767].

[67] Ibid.

- **Learn from the Millennials.**

*"I believe that my [M]illennial peers and I are EXTREMELY savvy when it comes to technology. I think this can be both a negative and positive thing. I think it can be negative because we (the Millennials) expect that everyone in the organization will be on the same level as us and will have the same understanding of technology as we do. I've seen both myself and my peers get frustrated when their older superiors don't understand how complex a report was to produce because they don't know how to use the database or software that the report was built off of. Therefore, their superiors feel that they can make changes to their reports that are either impossible to make or extremely time consuming or unnecessary."*
Faryn Rosen (Millennial)
Talent Acquisition Specialist, HR OnProcess Technology

Palfrey and Gasser suggest in *Born Digital* that "parents and teachers need to let Digital Natives be their guides into this new, connected way of living."[68] Not only do I agree, and in fact believe that this has been happening in greater and greater frequency, but I also believe that organizations and managers should employ the same philosophy. We know that we have a lot to learn from our Millennial brethren, and probably nowhere more than with our implementation and usage of technology.

*"We believe [M]illennials bring a lot to our organization with their high productivity, curious creativity and technological savvy. They have a positive influence on other generations in our division, but they're also learning from and being mentored by [G]en [X]-ers, [B]oomers and [T]raditionalists."* (cont. on page 89)

---

[68] John Palfrey and Urs Gasser, *Born Digital: Understanding the First Generation of Digital Natives* (New York: Basic Books, 2008).

*(cont. from page 88)*

*"Capitalizing on the unique strengths of each generation also could lead to increased sales of our products. If we want to reach younger consumers, we must understand the appeal of text messaging and Facebook. Many intern projects this past summer involved working on 'intranet' home pages or sites for various departments that could provide training or efficiencies. We try to use this to Hallmark and the intern's advantage. In college relations, a [M]illennial employee is currently creating a Facebook page for our new Hallmark interns in addition to opportunities to communicate with this group via text and provide just in time information."*
Julie Wille
College Recruiting Representative, Hallmark Cards

This requires an understanding of how Millennials use technology, and an appreciation of the fact that their way with technology may be different from those of us who are X-ers or Boomers. All too often we find ourselves making judgments about just how engaged a younger colleague is in the conversation or activity, readily dismissing the possibility that they actually could be connecting with us while still being tuned in to whatever media device they are simultaneously hooked up to at that moment. I'll be honest – I often need convincing of this, and frequently question just how effective multi-tasking is.

*"For me, I would say that the most negative consequence of a Millennial employee is the inability to stay focused on a given task. Distraction is the rule rather than the exception. When directing them to perform tasks that might involve some research on the web, I look up to find them checking their Hotmail and reading about the latest technological innovations. I must continuously inquire about their status to bring their focus back to the task."*
R. Kyle Jones
Founder and Principle, EduSophia

I also am concerned as I discover more information about what impact information overload has on the human psyche. "Multitasking tends to be bad for learning (though there are a few exceptions). According to psychologists, kids learn better if they pay full attention to the things they want to remember. Recently, the adverse effect of multitasking on children's ability to learn new facts and concepts has been supported by brain-imaging studies."[69] I don't think that children are the only ones who are susceptible to this, and it is also critical to remember that our new Millennial employees were for the most part reared amidst this digital revolution, and are self-proclaimed ultimate multi-taskers. But despite a commonly held idea that the electronics in our world help to ease our stress, "actually, the opposite is true: paying too much attention to the TV, computer, or Blackberry adds to your anxiety levels..., says [Sandra Bond] Chapman."[70] They maintain that they are great multi-taskers and that it in fact helps them to keep up with it all. While I may have concern about the quality of their work or output, as they dip in and of out of multiple things at once, I have to appreciate their own experience of themselves, as well as the experience of some (though not all) of their managers.

> *"The biggest challenge is helping the more senior professionals understand that these newer hires can still be extremely productive and engaged even though they are multi-tasking (i.e. IMing, texting, or listening to their iPods while doing project work)."*
> Cindi Rotondo
> National University Recruiting Manager, Navigant Consulting, Inc.

As Palfrey and Gasser discuss, "[t]he Jury is still out on whether the higher levels of distraction associated with multitasking are outweighed by the overall gains in productivity from their use of digital technologies."[71]

> *"I do not believe their ability to communicate face to face with others has suffered as a result of technology. In fact, through the constant communication of email, text, and instant messaging, I believe Millennials have developed strong communication skills."*
> *(cont. on page 91)*

---

[69] Ibid.

[70] Charlotte Latvala, "De-Stress Your Weeknights," *Good Housekeeping Magazine*, January 2009.

[71] Ibid.

*(cont. from page 90)*

*"By deciphering feelings from the short phrases of text or instant messaging, Millennials are able to infer or read into what others might implicitly be telling them. They are able to comprehend and lead nuanced communications. They just developed these skills differently than previous generations.*

*"Because they can leverage technology, Millennials work quicker and smarter than their peers. Millennials will spend more time planning and analyzing work and less time doing it than other workers. The time to collect data and generate reports is reduced by the utilization of technology. For instance, in MS Excel, Millennials will create whole reports that rely on layered formulas, while older workers might feel that they do not trust the formula function and take much longer completing the report with a calculator, and less time analyzing the data."*

Seth Nable
Manager Training and Development
Human Resources OnProcess Technology

- **Capitalize on their knowledge and use it to bring the organization forward.**

Millennials have technological skills and knowledge that can bring tremendous benefit to the organization. There are fantastic opportunities to enhance efficiencies and, in turn, profits, and Millennials can help us to develop them.

*"We have yet to see anything negative about their tech savvy ways. In fact, they are able to drill down to their 'work' faster because they're spending less time on figuring the technology out. Their ability to multi-task on various technology platforms is on one hand amazing, but at times we worry if they can truly focus with so many things to tend to. The true benefit for us is how they are able to see our current work through fresh eyes - they can see an easier way to do something or see how our work can be leveraged through current technology."*

Helen Hong
College Relations Manager, WellPoint Inc.

> *"The [M]illennials advanced technical skills relate very well to analytical positions in most organizations. Their ability to sort and organize data using technology produces faster results and creates more efficiencies. They always look for a way to improve an existing process to make it more efficient and productive. Organizations love this because any time or cost savings can then be passed on to the customers."*
>
> Matt Duren
> College Recruiting Manager, GEICO

It is essential for the growth of our organizations that we capture this knowledge base and utilize it to keep our companies growing. Throughout time, it has been the implementation of new ideas and technologies that help to keep companies current and legitimate in a constantly shifting worldwide marketplace.

> *"We have noted that Millennials take a more active role in advocating for technology. They are willing to join taskforces to help the network move forward in this important area. Millennials have a strong presence on our technology taskforce, intranet development taskforce and 'Going-Green' taskforce."*
>
> Jules Feiman, Director of Human Resources
> YAI / National Institute for People with Disabilities Network

History is replete with cases of companies that folded due to lack of vision, or at least a lack of ability to shift and change as consumer demands morph. Millennials can provide new ideas and the new technologies to fulfill those ideas if we give them voice in our companies and really value what they have to offer, instead of dismissing them as the new crop of employees who need to do little more than listen and learn, while fulfilling only what is assigned to them and keeping their mouths shut.

> *"We have an extensive e-university platform for learning on-line; we've developed tools for internal networking and sharing. We have become much more comfortable with virtual meetings and use webinars, podcasts, and simulcasts to communicate and get project work done."*
>
> Irene DeNigris
> Director, Global University Recruitment Johnson & Johnson

- **Create "reverse mentoring" programs.**

Through the utilization of organized programs, opportunity for education and training of older workers can be effected while providing something that Millennials deeply crave: validation. It is clear that many Gen-X and, especially, Boomer employees have a lot of room for growth and improvement in their understanding and employment of technology in day-to-day work. Who better than new Millennial co-workers – or even supervisees – to help develop them in this area? We need to exploit this knowledge for the staying power of both the company and the employee. And the Millennial will not feel offended by this "exploitation;" Millennials thirst for this affirmation.

*"I have also seen this be a positive thing because Millennials at my company, myself included, can help to teach and educate their older co-workers or superiors on technology. If my boss is having difficulty with something on his PC, he always asks me for help! I think it's a great opportunity for me to help my boss and show him the value I can add to not only the company but also to him and his job. It is also a positive thing because Millennials know that we can rely on one another to help us with any technology-related question. If I get stuck on something or have a problem within a database, I never have to look too far to find someone that can help me solve the problem."*
Faryn Rosen (Millennial)
Talent Acquisition Specialist, HR OnProcess Technology

Of course, some of this education will come from general interaction and interfacing in the workplace, a natural outcome of everyday interfacing on work issues and other collegial interactions.

*"We've used interns to assist in bringing older workers into the technology realm via text-messaging, IM, etc. While these technologies are inherent to students, many older workers don't have a network using these technologies so they lack the skills to adeptly ingrain them into daily work habits. Our more youthful interns assist in overcoming this issue by forcing these tools into everyday worklife."*
Mason Gates
President, Internships.com

This does not mean that there is not substantial room for well-established systemic programs that provide this kind of structured teaching by the newer employee to the more seasoned employee. Some companies are already pursuing this kind of program, but more should. "Of course, young people have always helped their parents and grandparents brush up on pop culture or how to use the latest technology gizmo. And brash, young workers have always felt they know more than management — at least when it comes to their job. But reverse mentoring ratchets up the concept a notch or two. In recent years, a slew of companies have recognized its value and established reverse mentoring programs. The list includes General Electric, Proctor & Gamble, Philip Morris, Best Buy, Siemens and Chase Manhattan Bank. In addition, the Seattle Public Schools and the Wharton School of Business at the University of Pennsylvania have shifted the knowledge flow into reverse. Most observers credit former General Electric CEO Jack Welch as the catalyst for this burgeoning movement. Although the roots of corporate reverse mentoring extend back to the early 1990s, it wasn't until the end of the decade that the high-profile chief executive ordered 500 of his top managers to find workers who could teach them the finer points of Web browsing and researching online. Welch himself choose a mentor and blocked off time to learn about everything from browser bookmarks to competitors' Web sites. Prior to that, Welch had rarely surfed the Web and found himself overwhelmed by the experience."[72]

- **Educate the entire workforce on generational differences.**

It is clear that education will be key in supporting the effective work of a cross-generational workplace. Millennials need to understand the mindset and experiences of older employees, just as the older employees need to develop a better understanding of their new young colleagues. The goal is to develop appreciation, and even tolerance, amidst these groups with such different psychologies and outlooks – without this, there is a risk to the collaboration that often needs to occur in today's professional environment.

*"It is important to provide classes on generational differences to companies."*
Maren Mercado
Human Resources Generalist, McGladrey & Pullen

---

[72] Samuel Greengard, "Learning in Reverse," *The Galt Global Review*, September 23, 2003, 12/27/08 [http://www.galtglobalreview.com/education/learning_in_reverse.html].

*"To better connect the different generation in our workforce, Duke has initiated a program here called 'Lunch and Learn.'... It is an opportunity for an informal "information change and networking". We have topics about new technology, new forms of communication, and changes within the workplace. Each 'Lunch and Learn' is presented by varying employees within the varying generations here at Duke. Our goal is to bring people, products, and ideas together to form a better workplace!"*
Bill Phillips
Sr. Recruiting Specialist
(Strategic Talent Development), Duke Energy Corporation

Unfortunately, seminars and programs such as these are not always possible for every company, and it also raises the question, when should they be done? Companies, particularly larger ones, experience lots of turnover given the size of the organization, so do you hold seminars on this topic once each month? Once every six months? Once a year? What is the right formula to ensure that people continue to be appropriately educated? Certainly it is imperative to supplement these with a tangible resource that can be used as a reference tool – or a vehicle for ongoing discussion – for employees and managers. There are a small number of companies that have begun adding to their organizational manuals to address cross-generational issues in the workplace, but it is very few who have tackled this. It is a broad step to enhance an employee manual – traditionally a resource for company policies and protocols – in this way, but this is another example of the way the times are changing.

*"My plan for the coming year is to provide a manual to all intern/ entry level hiring managers, including a section on how to 'deal' with the generation."*
Anonymous
Recruiter, Retailer

I believe that there may be no area that has more profoundly impacted the development of Millennials and influences how they interface at work and really in all aspects of their lives. There are, as I like to say and as I have discussed at great length through this chapter, both highlights and hurdles when we look at Millennials and technology.

*"Today's generation in general is much more technologically savvy than those from the past. From text messaging, to newer software, to the replacement of face to face meetings with emails and video conferencing, the Millennial Generation definitely walks to the beat of a different drummer. A lot of the older generation are not as quick to buy into this new age way of thinking and sometimes this causes a disconnect within the workforce. For instance, take emailing and text messaging[:] a Millennial may shoot a text message or email something rather than leave a voicemail or schedule a face to face meeting. This disconnect has caused issues with relationship building. With better education on both sides, we can bridge this gap by helping each have a better understanding of the other. Regarding new software, the Millennial is much quicker to pick things up. Some may view this as an asset; some may view it as a negative. It can be viewed as a negative if the manager feels threatened that his new employees pick up on things faster. Some managers, however, treat it as a bonus for having employees who are quick learners or know the software already."*

Bill Phillips
Sr. Recruiting Specialist (Strategic Talent Development)
Duke Energy Corporation

Clearly, older generations are often really challenged by this whole new outlook and lifestyle with regard to technology. The oft-discussed "generation gap" probably stands out more around technology than anything else – as has probably been true for all generations throughout time. And one of the environments where it stands out is, of course, the workplace. Without a doubt, the way to minimize the downside and capitalize on the upside involves clear recognition and understanding of how these differences come into play, and the development of strong and effective education and training to help develop all generations in the workplace around these issues. The key to organizational survival is adaptation to "Generation 2.0."

• The social interactions, friendships, and various other activities of Millennials are dramatically impacted by their use of digital technologies. Growing up amidst a digital revolution has informed the ways in which Millennials relate to each other, people of other generations, and their surrounding world.

• With more spent interfacing with television and other forms of media, less time has been spent doing traditionally creative activities, or engaging in imaginative thought or play. As a result, this generation may have less developed creative skills, though there are arguments to be made for the ways in which technology has not only enabled, but really inspired, a whole new creative art form.

• Millennials' lifelong experience playing and experimenting with so many forms of technology help them to be exceedingly comfortable figuring things out, designing new programs or websites, and using online communities to enhance their workplaces. Companies have a lot to gain from the efficiencies that Millennials bring to the workplace through the creative employment of technology.

• An unintended consequence of the Millennial Generation's experience of immediacy that technology has always provided to them, is that they struggle with exhibiting patience and sitting with uncertainty. While technology is a major tool for Millennials in their efforts to "multi-task" as they remain busy at all times, there are many that question of the efficacy of multi-tasking. Another consequences of immediacy may be that Millennials are impatient about a lot of things; employers see that they don't always spend the time needed to get the job "done right" because they want to get on to the next thing. And further, they are impatient – and, as a result, unrealistic – with their own career advancement.

• Educators have been concerned for years about the impact of technology on this generation's communication abilities, and this issue has begun to have ramifications as they arrive in the workplace. Millennials' deficient skills in written communication has been a cause of concern for supervisors, as has been the issue of appropriate usage of technology; supervisors find increased problems with this generation – despite directives to the contrary – utilizing work technology for personal purposes. *(cont. on page 98)*

## CHAPTER THREE: SUMMARY (continued)

• The lifelong experience of being "hooked in" to one form of media or another results in a lack of time spent in actual reflection. Millennials often report that they do not allow themselves the time to reflect, as they are always too busy rushing from one thing to the next, or filling their time with all that technology has to offer. It is apparent that they come to the workplace with some underdeveloped critical life skills as a result, and further that they are unpracticed at taking time to think and process – essential skills for an effective employee.

• Organizations may be able to respond to these issues with the enhancement of existing leadership development programs that aim to teach this new generation of employees everything from issues of workplace technology etiquette to proper professional communication. Companies need to be willing to invest in technology upgrades, as the quality of technology within the organization will be a major factor in where the Millennial candidate chooses to go to work. And Millennials have a lot to offer to the organization with their expertise in this area, and this should be capitalized upon by capturing their knowledge base and developing reverse-mentorship programs that enable Millennials to teach older colleagues how to better utilize technology.

# CHAPTER FOUR

## Millennials - The Programmed Generation?

**M**illennials are extraordinarily active, and much of this activity takes place in a group setting of one sort or another, including virtual groups. They have been raised learning, playing, working, and being evaluated in groups, and they are well tuned to team-orientation. In his 2001 article, "The Organization Kid," David Brooks described the very full days of the college students that he interviewed: "I asked several students to describe their daily schedules, and their replies sounded like a session of Future Workaholics of America: crew practice at dawn, classes in the morning, resident-adviser duty, lunch, study groups, classes in the afternoon, tutoring disadvantaged kids in Trenton, a cappella practice, dinner, study, science lab, prayer session, hit the StairMaster, study a few hours more."[73] In stark contrast to the current economic situation, Brooks wrote this article at a time when these college students were not so involved solely to pad resumes to be more marketable in a difficult hiring environment, but because they found personal value in it. "An activity—whether it is studying, hitting the treadmill, drama group, community service, or one of the student groups they found and join in great numbers—is rarely an end in itself. It is a means for self-improvement, résumé-building, and enrichment."[74] This was nothing new to those of us who work with college students and young adults. As a tremendously busy college administrator, I still find that it is sometimes harder for students to find time in their schedules to meet with me than it is for me to find the time to meet with them! And it isn't new; Millennials have been this way for most of their lives, moving from one structured activity to the next.

---

[73] David Brooks, "The Organization Kid," *The Atlantic*, April 2001.

[74] Ibid.

> *"I have always grown up working in teams. Both at the High School level and College level I was always immersed in team activities, writing team papers, even taking tests in teams! I am fortunate that at my current company we also rely heavily on our 'teams' (departments) to help us with our work. Although we do a lot of independent work, we also have a lot of opportunity to work with others within our departments and other areas of the company."*
> Faryn Rosen (Millennial)
> Talent Acquisition Specialist, Human Resources OnProcess Technology

There has been much made over the years of the phenomena of "hyper-scheduling," with evidence on all sides about the positive and negative consequences of so many arranged group-based activities. There is, of course, great value to all of this teaming, with people learning to work cooperatively and towards common goals starting in childhood. Further, "[t]here is quite consistent and strong evidence of a positive association between participating in organized activities and a variety of indicators of positive development: those youth who participate demonstrate healthier functioning on such indicators ranging from academic achievement, school completion, post secondary educational attainment, psychological adjustment, and lowered rates of smoking and drug use, to the quantity and quality of interactions with their parents."[75] It is believed that the hectic quality of their lives has made them accustomed to working from schedules and following rules, and, as a result, they are used to being assessed, receiving focused feedback, and being goal-directed. Having participated in group-projects at school, they are team-oriented, socially networked, and able to organize and mobilize.[76] Colleges have long capitalized on the team-orientation of the generation, recognizing their propensity for congregation and cooperation, building these skill sets further, hopefully preparing them for the collaborative nature of many work settings. This is all quite good news for the managers and supervisors of these young people now that they have grown into adulthood.

---

[75] Joseph L. Mahoney, Angel L. Harris, & Jacquelynne S. Eccles, "Organized Activity Participation, Positive Youth Development, and the Over-Scheduling Hypothesis," *Social Policy Report: Giving Child and Youth Development Knowledge Away*, 2006.

[76] Robert DeBard, "Millennials Coming to College," *Serving the Millennial Generation (New Directions for Student Services)*. Ed. Michael D. Coomed and Robert DeBard. California: 2004.

*"I agree that Millennials are more team-oriented than other groups – especially since they spent most of their schooling in environments that centered around team learning. They love challenges and insist on 'meaningful' work. Managers and co-workers would hear it immediately if Millennials were not being challenged or fully utilized during their employment. This generation is not shy to voice their dissatisfaction of certain job elements to their supervisors. Even though they are effective at multi-tasking, they seem to need structure and would in most cases need team goals broken down into specific steps.*

*I always found it interesting that they feel comfortable in a team-oriented environment but our marketing efforts were always targeting them as unique and 'special' individuals (i.e. We had 'My Career' sites, 'MySpace,' 'YouTube,' etc. I think the key message was that we needed to balance their specific needs – but ensured we were portraying a collaborative and fun working environment."*

Tara Place
HR/College Relations, financial service industry

Most organizations have grown over recent years, regardless of the generational composition of their employees, to recognize the benefit of teaming for projects, and Millennials have fit quite nicely into this business practice.

*"Our organization has always been very team-oriented. Many of the [M]illennials that come in to our organization say they enjoy this aspect of working at GEICO. We celebrate the success of teams that accomplish great things, but it does not stop there. We also celebrate the accomplishments and successes of individuals as a team. To GEICO, this isn't new, this is our culture."*

Matt Duren
College Recruiting Manager, GEICO

Unfortunately, there also comes a downside with these advantages. While research on organized activities has shown more positive consequences, on balance, of participation for academic, educational, social, civic, and physical development[77], there has been a great deal written about the impact of this busy lifestyle on a developing young person. I have serious concerns about the lack of time for and emphasis on any kind of contemplation, which I strongly believe hinders the development not only of critical thinking and analytical skills, but also of necessary coping mechanisms. And I am not alone in this unrest. "'They've just got so much more on their plates,' says Karen, 45, a scientist with the Environmental Protection Agency (EPA). 'I don't remember ever being under as much pressure.' ... 'I don't want to discourage them from being active and doing well in school, but I'm really concerned about them suffering from burnout,' says Matt, 48, who also works as an EPA regulator. 'And I don't want them to miss out on us spending time together as a family.' Karen worries that her children's lifestyle leaves too little room for imagination and curiosity, let alone fun. 'When we were kids, we'd pick up a rock and wonder why it looked the way it did,' she says. 'Nobody has the time to do that now -- unless they're in geology camp.'"[78] Karen and Matt may be parents of younger kids, but their children's experience is not so different from that of our Millennial workers as they were growing up. And many of them found that they did – and continue to – pay a price for their stress.

*"While I was in middle school and high school, I was always in the honors courses, star of the cross country and track team, peer mediator, student council, vice president, and the list goes on. I snapped. I fell into the wrong crowd and dropped out of school leaving all of that pressure behind me. Because I was a smart person and had a lot of support (which I did not accept right off the bat) I got out of the hole I had dug, went back to high school and graduated college. I remember my dad telling me to take it easy, don't take on so much, but the school said different. I had to not only keep up with everyone around me, but do better than them. It all worked out in the end, but not the way I always thought it would."*

Lindsay Shields (Millennial)
Client Services Account Specialist
Human Resources OnProcess Technology

---

[77] Joseph L. Mahoney, Angel L. Harris, & Jacquelynne S. Eccles, "Organized Activity Participation, Positive Youth Development, and the Over-Scheduling Hypothesis" *Social Policy Report: Giving Child and Youth Development Knowledge Away*, 2006.

[78] Patrick Kiger, "Today's Overscheduled Kids," *Ladies Home Journal*, June 2004.

Researchers have found continued consequences of these childhood pressures. "A 2003 study of 649 college students by sociologists Heather Turner and Melissa Butler at the University of New Hampshire found that childhood stress was a significant factor in young-adult depression, and other research has confirmed the link. Sharon Post, a family therapist in San Jose, California, worries that today's stressed-out kids will turn into a generation of emotionally damaged adults. Kids who've grown up being pressured to overachieve grow into confused, alienated young adults, says Post. 'Their sense of worth will come from what they do, rather than who they are. They won't know who they really are.'"[79] I have certainly found in my research that the Millennial Generation has seriously underdeveloped coping mechanisms, and I believe a huge factor in this is that they have not been allowed the "luxury" of time to think, feel, and process – essential ingredients for psychological and emotional development. Madeline Levine writes, "many kids find themselves scheduled to within an inch of their lives. Criticism and even rejection become commonplace as competitive parents continue to push their children towards higher levels of accomplishment. As a result, kids can't find the time, both literal and psychological, to linger in internal exploration; a necessary precursor to a well-developed sense of self."[80]

Yet another consequence of such rigorously structured programming is a lack of creative and leadership development. Millennials are a generation raised in structured activities, always organized, presented, and presided over by adults. As a child, I remember being able to go out after dinner and find other kids playing in the neighborhood; we would come up with our own games, creating rules and structures for them. These activities were not engineered or directed by adults; in fact, rarely were parents present. With this independence and freedom, conflict arose and was then resolved, inquisitiveness was fostered, and true cooperation skills were built. Parents and teachers were not present to intervene and solve, and children had to rely upon their internal skills sets and resiliency. This is not to say that there were no "Lord of the Flies" phenomena that occurred, but there is a lot of benefit to this autonomy that lacked for Millennials in their youth.

---

[79] Ibid.

[80] Madeline Levine, Ph.D., *The Price of Privilege: How Parental Pressure and Material Advantage Are Creating a Generation of Disconnected and Unhappy Kids* (New York: HarperCollins Publishers, 2006).

> *"We are a non-profit organization and are usually understaffed. We work in groups on a variety of levels on a regular basis. I have found that these employees are more willing to work in groups and share credit; however, they need more direction about the division of labor, the leadership and the goals. Along the way the management is involved much more. They struggle with working independently."*
> Anonymous
> Assistant Director, Career Development Non-Profit Organization

"Contrary to the widely held belief that only intellectual activities build a sharp brain, it's in play that the cognitive skills are the most acutely developed. By play I'm referring not to adult-coached and adult-monitored sports, but to true play: free, unstructured play, where kids invent the activities, the activities reflect their own curiosity and interests – and they can find their own ways to be with each other. ... Child's play fosters decision making, memory, thinking, and speed of mental processing. ... Play sharpens wits and makes mental processes nimble – resilient and ready for whatever life throws our way."[81] By overseeing too much of our children's experiences, are we hindering some crucial development? Are we even, with so many adult-supervised activities, hampering team-orientation, since they are constantly being instructed on how to be a team player instead of allowed to build the quality themselves?

> *"I have found Millennials to have an 'out for myself' attitude or an attitude of it's not my job or in my job description so I am not going to do it, in spite of the fact that it might be the best thing for the organization, or the client or those we serve. My experience has been that they often don't understand the real meaning of team player, greater good, and working toward a common goal. They see much more and strive much more for personal success (promotion, raises, bonuses, and pats on the back) than they do organizational successes (securing a grant, meeting program goals, media and press coverage, attendance at an event, etc...)."*
> Sharon Zimmerman
> Deputy Director, WAND (Women's Action for New Directions)
> (formerly Vice President for Programs and Services, Goodwill Industries)

---

[81] Hara Estroff Marano, *A Nation of Wimps: The High Cost of Invasive Parenting* (New York: Broadway Books, 2008).

Of course, as I've discussed before, not every Millennial has been raised with so much activity and programming. Many could not afford the costs of all of these activities, making this a problem of the more entitled in our society – an "affluenza" of sorts. While Judith Walker, in her *New York Times* article on this phenomena, "Camp Codependence," explains that wealth is not a pre-requisite to affluenza, there is a diminished susceptibility for those of more meager means. She notes that while several studies have shown positive trending with American teenagers in recent decades around issues such as teen suicide, pregnancy, substance use and violence, upper-middle-class kids still appear to be surpassing their peers in rates of cigarette smoking, depression, alcohol and drug abuse, anxiety, rule-breaking, and psychosomatic disorders like headaches and stomach problems. Walker discusses the work of sociologist Annette Lareau, who found that working class children, "who have fewer scheduled activities, more unstructured time and less fussing-over generally by adults, are more spontaneous and creative in their play than are middle- and upper-middle-class kids, enjoy their leisure activities more, and show greater autonomy and self-reliance."[82]

I am not sure it is simply a matter of finances, either. Many parents lament the fact that while they don't necessarily want their kids to have a different activity almost every day of the week, that is where the other kids are. If my eight-year-old niece Sara wants to see her friends, she – and her parents – can find them at after-school soccer, not hanging out at the local playground.

There is certainly a range of behavioral and attitudinal outcomes that stem from Millennials' participatory experience. As they have come to work at our various companies and organizations, we have seen the impact of this aspect of their development, both the positive and the negative.

For the most part, Millennials team-orientation fits in well with organizations that have already placed a high value on this quality, and in many cases this has helped organizations to evolve further.

---

[82] Judith Warner, "Camp Codependence," *The New York Times*, July 31, 2008.

> *"Hallmark has a culture of being team-oriented, but everyone is still accountable for their own performance. Most departments are team- oriented and work together to reach common goals. If anything, the Millennials have probably helped to bridge this gap in departments. Many of our interns ask to work with each other on projects and that has happened in a few of our departments, which has been very successful. We also provide some small-scale Millennial training to intern managers so they are prepared if they have not done research. Some managers took it as opportunities to have the interns present to diversity councils on the different generations in the Hallmark workplace and what improvements can be made to achieve the common goals for the company."*
> Julie Wille
> College Recruiting Representative, Hallmark Cards

Aaron Green, Founder and President of Professional Staffing Group and PSG Offshore Resources, writes "[c]ritics of Gen Y believe that their dependency on their parents during youth would create friction and lack of responsibility in the workplace as adults. This concern has proven to be unwarranted. In fact, Millennials are superior team players. Whatever they supposedly lack in independence, Millennials make up for with a high level of aptitude for working in teams. From soccer camp to student council, they've been taught the importance of working in teams from day one and they will bring these values into their places of employment. Gen Y'ers are known to be social and outgoing, and these characteristics have brought teamwork in the office to a whole new level."[83] Whether Mr. Green's hypothesis is correct or not, if you want to capitalize on the strengths of their lifelong experience of constant structured activity while managing its consequences, **what organizational initiatives should you employ?**

- **Program, program, program.**

Let's recap here. Millennials have been raised with a culture of programming and activity. It is what they know and what they understand. The introduction of structured group-based programs that emulate those that they are used to can provide for them a concrete validation of the organization. The provision of a "leadership program" in which they can

---

[83] Aaron Green, "What do Millennials Teach Us About the Future of the Workplace," *The Boston Globe HR Center On Staffing*, May 19, 2008 [http://www.boston.com/jobs/on_staffing/051908.shtml].

participate tells them that the company is looking out for them and is enabling their professional development and opportunity for growth within the organization.

> *"We have absolutely seen this manifest within the work place and have tried to adapt through programs and offerings. For Example: at the graduate and undergraduate level, we began college hire programs that are 'Leadership Development Programs' – where new hires come in as classes – which have helped to create a sense of community that is formally carried through for the first two years of their employment. We have also experimented with new technologies – last year we developed an exciting new platform/tool for our global MBA population blending social networking and a 3-D world (think Second Life); this pilot was developed to bring a sense of community and engagement globally to our MBA hires."*
>
> Irene DeNigris
> Director, Global University Recruitment Johnson & Johnson

As I've said at other points, leadership and/or management training programs are not new; what may be different are their value for those who are participating. Again, it not only suggests the valuing of the employee, but it also enhances intra-organizational communication and business practices.

> *"We are definitely team-oriented. Our world is all about instant gratification and efficiency, so putting our brains together in team helps us to achieve just that! My company has evolved to be more team oriented. We call it 'interdependence.' Traditionally, in the financial industry, employees were very independent. They could do it all on their own and be successful. In today's world, there is just too much information. Clients are smarter. They ask more questions and there are so many options! One person can't handle this information overload, so they work in a team where each person can specialize in what they do best and leverage their teammates to be more successful as a whole and individually."*
>
> Becky Girola (Millennial)
> Director of Recruiting
> Northwestern Mutual Financial Network

- **Recognize "virtual" teamwork.**

> *"Because our organization is located in 14 different states and in multiple offices in different cities, we have to learn to work virtually; therefore, the team element is key to getting things done. We collaborate in cross-functional and department-specific teams throughout the enterprise, and it's been an asset to have Millennials already come with the mindset of working within a team. I find that they tend to be participatory and fully engaged in the work when they feel that they are making an impact. They also come with more developed relational skills, having been on group projects all throughout college."*
>
> Helen Hong
> College Relations Manager, WellPoint Inc.

Technology has a major role to play here. Millennials actually have substantial experience teaming with one another while never being in the same room, or even on the same continent. While I may think a conversation is something that can only take place between people who are in direct proximity to one another (or at least on the phone hearing each other's voice), Millennials cannot disagree more. They converse – not just communicate – via e-mail, text messages, IM'ing, Facebook, and every other tech medium imaginable. Believe it or not, on college campuses we see roommates sitting in the same dorm room sending each other text messages and IM's to communicate. This is not because they are fighting and don't want to talk; this *is* how they talk! As Mark Edmundson, Professor of English at the University of Virginia, wrote for *The Chronicle Review*, in March 2008, "[i]nternet technology was on hand for my current students from about the time they were eight years old; it was in 1995 that the Netscape browser made the Internet accessible to everyone. And the Internet seems to me to have shaped their generation as much as the multichannel TV, with that critical device, the remote control, shaped the students who registered for my classes a decade ago."[84] In fact, many "teen" activities in which Millennials engaged – and perhaps still engage – that we view as being isolated, like online gaming, are actually highly networked, team-based activities. We may think that young Johnny was remote and withdrawn when he spent so much time on his computer playing

---

[84] Mark Edmundson, "Dwelling in Possibility," *The Chronicle Review*, March 14, 2008.

games, but in fact he was engaged in collaborative and cooperative group activity that just happened to take place online. The internet has changed Millennials' view of working together; it stands to reason that Millennials, in turn, effect change in workplace teaming as a result.

> *"The Millennial Generation is also very interested in being networked within the company. Things we have done to increase networking opportunities include: [the] creation of an Intern/Co-op STUDENT ONLY SharePoint site. With MySpace and Facebook being blocked by Corporate, it allows a location for students to post messages about lunches, concerts, community events, and even non-Duke sponsored parties and gatherings. Postings have to be approved by our Recruiting/Staffing Intern. Anything borderline will be sent through a member of our Co-op/Intern Recruiting team to ensure it complies with company policy. The aforementioned Associates Programs have inter-company events, recreational leagues, and competitions. (This could be potentially where the group evaluations are seen...) The Millennial Generation seems to want to know what their peers are doing. ... I think the common denominator is that the Millennial Generation wants to be connected. They want to be connected to their company and more importantly their peers!"*
> Bill Phillips, Sr. Recruiting Specialist
> (Strategic Talent Development), Duke Energy Corporation

- **Consider physical layout.**

Capitalizing upon Millennials' orientation towards collaboration can be accomplished by something as simple as physically placing them in specific configurations.

> *"Learning circles; Gen Y gathers in small groups and talking about specific issues. Interns might do group projects in teams of four. They love sharing ideas [in this setting and] corporations are starting to respond. ... Millennials don't sit in cubes; they have huge open seating areas. Social networking is huge. [They n]eed to collaborate and need to be in a team (wiki is great, Facebook for recruiters, etc.), [As are r]eal-time webinars."*
> Alexandra Levitt
> Author, *How'd You Score That Gig*, Millennial Workplace Consultant

It's not just about locating members of workgroups in close proximity to one another; a layout that provides open spaces set up for lots of people to come together for brainstorming sessions and other group-based work can be a critical element of a vibrant collaborative environment. The conference room meetings of generations past don't appeal so much to the Millennials, and can interfere with cooperative group processes.

- **Really do it.**

Like with anything, the organization needs to put its money where its mouth is. Not surprisingly, it is not enough to talk a good game when it comes to valuing and promoting teamwork in the work environment, but this is where most organizations fall apart. It's not hard to imagine it: the prospective young employee talks during their interview about how important an open and collaborative work environment is to her, how collegial she is and how she is seeking just that kind of organization for her first job. Her prospective supervisor, in all honesty, talks about how aligned that outlook is with the organizational philosophy, describing the value placed on building effective teams and even employing participatory decision-making. And then what happens when the new employee begins work? She sees that everyone within the organization does share this value system, and they all even seem to believe that the company embodies that ideology, but the reality doesn't quite match up with everyone's perceptions. She thinks that perhaps "the emperor has no clothes!"

> *"I like that I am part of a team here, but I do not really work with the team as much as I would like. We are all very spread out because we all handle different parts of the whole process. Perhaps meeting with your team on a more regular basis [is the answer]. They talk about it, but it is never really put into effect. It is left up to each individual to meet with their team, but if I was to act on it, I think I would be the only one. If it's not something you have to do, many people do not do it."*
> Lindsay Shields (Millennial)
> Client Services Account Specialist, HR OnProcess Technology

- **Implement Developmental Supervision.**

If nothing else, Millennials are in need of mentorship and guidance that will help them to further develop skill sets that may need work. While this generation is smart and talented, they are too accustomed to having their existence managed by others, usually in group activities. From the time they woke up until the time they went to sleep, many Millennials have had their every activity organized for them, and delivered to them by their well-meaning parents and other adults. This has its consequences. They are not as capable of self-direction, and in the work environment, they have a lot of trouble with autonomy,

> *"Millennials want a lot of responsibility, but when they are left alone they procrastinate, they have trouble focusing. They need team atmosphere to egg them on, sense of accomplishment when things go well. Facilitated teams are becoming very common."*
> Alexandra Levitt
> Author, *How'd You Score That Gig*, Millennial Workplace Consultant

In consulting with various organizations on working with their new Millennial employees, I have stressed the need to provide concrete direction that develops independence in the employee. This is a difficult but crucial supervisory talent, developing the employee as a stronger worker over time. It takes patience and creativity on the part of the manager to teach the employee how to be self-directed, but for the employee's professional growth and ability to take on more within the organization, it is most essential.

> *"The Millennials in our company I feel definitely need more guidance, they are so literal, and do only what is asked. Trying to teach them to look beyond the immediate easy answer and delve further and deliver more in-depth information is a challenge. Here we haven't changed anything, our challenge is to educate these individuals to look beyond their immediate answer, see if there are other resources with different perspectives or more in-depth info. What we find is that when the Millennials are asked to source info, a lot of the info is coming from the same source."*
> Anonymous
> HR/Professional Development, Financial Service Industry

Some of this can be achieved by simply moving from supervisory meetings, where the boss gives a list of "to-do's" to the worker, to ones where the employee comes in prepared to explain planned next steps him or herself. Another great tool is asking the employee to embark on their own

SWOT Analysis (Strengths, Weaknesses, Opportunities, Threats) of a situation, and ask them to come up with a feasible action plan. These tactics are not necessarily new, – many companies have been employing them with workers for some time – but now more than ever is this kind of developmental supervision important. And many managers are ill-equipped to deal with the underdeveloped self-sufficiency of the new generation of employees, and in fact need some coaching and development themselves. Certainly many Millennials see their superiors struggling to manage their needs and professional development.

*"We have a leadership program for young people coming into the company, but I think a leadership program for the managers would be extremely helpful. As a young, growing company, I know that it can be difficult to fill positions as fast as we need them, which forces us to place people in management positions who may not belong there. For this reason, these managers need to be trained. There are few who are born to be leaders, and even if you are a born leader, it is much different to be a manager. There are entire semester-long classes in college teaching students to be good managers. I believe that OnProcess could benefit from such programs."*
Lindsay Shields (Millennial)
Client Services Account Specialist, HR OnProcess Technology

Strauss and Howe saw evidence of Millennials' strong team-orientation even before the turn of the Millennium, noting "[f]irstborn Millennials are showing a clearer sense of generational membership earlier in their lifecycle than any other youths in American history, including Boomers and Gen X-ers. Around 1960, if anyone had asked Boomers whether they were part of a 'new generation,' the answer would have been 'huh?' In the late 70s, the media paid almost no attention to Gen X-ers, who, come their early-'90s discovery, often denied there was such a thing as Gen X. But when you ask that question of today's Millennials, you get a crisp, culturally informed answer – usually a 'yes.'"[85] Clearly, Millennials have a strong sense of group identification that has grown from a fairly consistent collective experience of assemblage and organization throughout their upbringing; they may be considered more of a "we versus me" generation. They

---

[85] Neil Howe and William Strauss, *Millennials Rising: The Next Great Generation* (New York: Vintage Books, 2000).

are used to hectic lives, activity after activity, most of it happening with groups of Millennial peers. Having virtually no experience with unstructured, unchoreographed time has influenced a lot of who they are and, for that matter, how they think and act – and now they are affecting their environs. The "Programmed Generation" has joined the workforce, and they are already having an influence.

## CHAPTER FOUR: SUMMARY

• Millennials have been raised with active, busy lives, and much of their activity has taken place in group settings, including virtual groups. They have been raised learning, playing, working, and being evaluated in groups, and they are well tuned to team-orientation.

• There has been strong value to their teaming, as Millennials have typically learned to work cooperatively and towards common goals starting in childhood, and organizations recognize their propensity for congregation and cooperation, capitalizing upon this skill set in the collaborative nature of many work settings.

• There are those who worry that these busy childhoods have created many "stressed-out kids" who will, in turn, develop into emotionally damaged adults. There is also concern that the rigorous structured programming may lead to a lack of creative and leadership development.

• Millennials are a generation raised in structured activities, always organized, presented, and presided over by adults. Without the experience of autonomy, Millennials may have less developed skills sets of conflict resolution and resiliency.

• The issues related to hyper-programming are more prevalent among the middle class or affluent in American society, and can be viewed as a form of "affluenza." Research suggests that working class children, who suffer less from with overscheduling and overly-involved parenting, are more spontaneous and creative, enjoy their leisure activities more, and show greater autonomy and self-reliance, than their middle- and upper-class peers.

• Millennials team-orientation fits in well with organizations that have already placed a high value on this quality, and this can help organizations to evolve further. *(cont. on page 114)*

## CHAPTER FOUR: SUMMARY (continued)

• Organizations can employ different initiatives that can capitalize on Millennials' team-orientation; these can include structured group-based leadership and professional development programs that emulate those that they are used to, which have the additional effect of providing to them a concrete validation of the organization. Further, through the use of social media technology, virtual workplace teaming may take on a whole new dimension with Millennial employees, and changing the physical layout of work spaces can have positive impact on the enhancement of a vibrant collaborative environment. Most importantly, Millennials are in need of mentorship and guidance that will help them to further develop skill sets that may need work, and developmental supervision is key to this endeavor.

# CHAPTER FIVE

## Millennials - The Celebrated Generation?

**Mrs. Incredible:**
I can't believe you don't want to go to your own son's graduation!

**Mr. Incredible:**
It's not a graduation. He is moving from the fourth grade to the fifth grade.

**Mrs. Incredible:**
It's a ceremony.

**Mr. Incredible:**
It's psychotic. They keep creating new ways to celebrate mediocrity, but if someone is genuinely exceptional, then it...

**Mrs. Incredible:**
This is not about you Bob!!

I love this scene from *The Incredibles!* I actually play it a lot when presenting to or consulting with groups about Millennials; it so perfectly captures many societal influences on the rearing of this generation. Please don't get me wrong here; I love those little kindergarten graduations as much as anybody. The kids are all lined up in their little paper caps and gowns, looking about as adorable as they possibly could! I actually don't really see anything wrong with any of these individual festivities and accolades, but I do see the cumulative effect of the constant outpouring of acknowledgement and reward. We have raised a new "celebrated generation" and it has its impact. They see it themselves.

> *"Growing up I was always praised and rewarded for a job well done. Whether it was a special shopping trip for good grades, or a big hug and a congratulations card from mom and dad when I got accepted into college, I became accustomed to being recognized for a special achievement, no matter how minor that achievement was."*
> Faryn Rosen (Millennial)
> Talent Acquisition Specialist, HR OnProcess Technology

They also recognize that they can and do adapt on this score, but find that it certainly takes some work.

> *"I have found myself upset at the fact that my boss hasn't recognized what a great job I do. Looking back on it though, she does recognize it and has told me 'good job' on a number of occasions, but I sometimes feel it is not enough. I hold resentments. When I discuss my feelings with my father (born 1956) he laughs at me and tells me that this is part of the working world. I agree with him and I am working towards accepting and understanding this. I want to be more accepting and less resentful. I am more than willing to be part of a team, and actually work well in teams much of the time. I do wonder, though, if some of this resentment comes from [different issues with] management rather than my need for a pat on the back. My goal is to overcome these negative feelings no matter where they come from and face the fact that the working world is a very different place than I am used to. There is a large mix of personalities, abilities, and ages that all have to come together and work as a team, and this is something I want to be a part of."*
> Lindsay Shields (Millennial)
> Client Services Account Specialist
> Human Resources OnProcess Technology

I am not alone with Mr. Incredible in my concern on this matter. In June 2008, *The New York Times* sparked a debate about the merit of elaborate eighth-grade graduations, "[w]hile some educators are grateful that notice is still being paid to academic achievement, others deride the festivities as overpraising what should be routine accomplishment. Some principals, school superintendents and legislators are trying to scale back the grandeur. But stepping between parents and ever-escalating celebrations of their children's achievements can be dicey, at best."[86] There are many arguments to be made for the benefit and value of acknowledging an accomplishment like finishing middle school, including the fact that for many children coming from unusually challenging home or personal environments, finishing eighth grade is in fact a tremendous accomplishment. But I feel that this is part of a larger picture of excess reward. Even Barack Obama – prior to the completion of his successful run for the Presidency – weighed in on this: "'Now hold on a second — this is just eighth grade,' he said. 'So, let's not go over the top. Let's not have a huge party. Let's just give them a handshake.' He continued: 'You're supposed to graduate from eighth grade.'"[87]

Is this where it all comes from? How have we, as a collective society, raised a generation that expects and craves constant praise and accolades? And what else comes with it? Are there positive aspects to this? Do Millennials have a robust sense of self and self-worth that should be appreciated, and perhaps emulated, by other generations?

*"Based on my experience working with and managing Millennials, I've found they are a group that definitely thrives on praise and recognition. Typically, they seem to embrace 'mentoring' and coaching – as opposed to some generations who perceive the support/help as a negative reflection on their work efforts.*

*"My previous employer [in the financial service industry] enhanced the ways of working with employees based on the Millennial generation. The Business units within [the organization] that rely heavily on entry level talent had to change their approach in attracting, retaining and developing this population of talent. For example, there was more focus on shared learning - through teams collaborating and sharing 'best practices' at staff meetings. Many teams would have 'star achievement' programs where folks were recognized at staff meetings for above and beyond work and provided gift certificates for their achievements."*

*(cont. on page 118)*

---

[86] Jan Hoffman, "Does 8th-Grade Pomp Fit the Circumstance?", *The New York Times*, June 22, 2008.

[87] Ibid.

*(cont. from page 117)*

*"Other groups would host 'great place to work' events – such as monthly team outings/lunches, etc. These social outings were looked at as opportunities for the staff to get to know each other better and build a stronger sense of community at work.*

*"Additionally, [the organization] would offer Manager trainings to those supervisors who would hire a significant number of entry-level or internship talent. The trainings would consist of tips on how to effectively manage this population – and would include the importance of having such programs as group outings/ achievement awards, etc."*

Tara Place

HR/College Relations, financial service industry

Not surprisingly, it seems to cut both ways, a topic addressed by Dr. Jean Twenge in *Generation Me: Why Today's Young Americans Are More Confident, Assertive, Entitled – and More Miserable Than Ever Before.* (Even the title talks to the very heart of this matter – a lifetime of positive attention and celebration may bring about confidence, but it comes with cost as well.) "Our childhoods of constant praise, self-esteem boosting, and unrealistic expectations did not prepare us for an increasingly competitive workplace and the economic squeeze created by sky-high housing prices and rapidly accelerating healthcare costs. After a childhood of buoyancy, GenMe is working harder to get less."[88] Take note that Twenge defines GenMe's birth span slightly differently than the time span that I and many generational researchers use to characterize Millennials; she actually creates a new generational "group" by overlapping the latter five or so years of Gen X with approximately the first 15 years attributed to Millennials. But Twenge does otherwise define GenMe much the way Millennials are frequently described, and discusses a lot of Strauss and Howe's theories in the process. She argues, as I do, that "young people should be seen as products of their culture – a culture that teaches them the primacy of the individual at virtually every step, and a culture that was firmly in place before they were born."[89] Millennials did not create the society that has

---

[88] Jean M. Twenge, PhD, *Generation Me: Why Today's Young Americans Are More Confident, Assertive, Entitled – and More Miserable Than Ever Before* (New York: Free Press, 2006).

[89] Ibid.

celebrated their every (non-)achievement; they are simply the outcome of it. And there are those who want a free pass from some of it. In a recent conversation with a professional acquaintance, Susan Kennedy of Career Treking, I was told about a really interesting conversation she had with her 11-year-old. It seems he has been taking diving lessons, and it turns out he actually has a real aptitude for it, so much so that the coach wanted to move him to a more advanced group. Susan wasn't particularly keen on this, as he already has lots of things in which he is involved, but she spoke with her son to see what he wanted to do. His response? "Why do I have to get good at everything, mom?" I was quite impressed by his mature and reflective response...out of the mouths of babes, I guess. But not all Millennials react in this way; in fact, I would suggest that most are quite caught up, first with the "help" of their parents and later, as they get older, of their own accord, with the "keeping up with the Joneses" doctrine that has increased with this generation. And we need to look at what impact it has had.

It is of course quite important to acknowledge that the recognition is not entirely misplaced, and further, it has contributed to very positive qualities for this collective group, not the least of which is that Millennials are confident. It is now "cool" to be smart, and they are indeed smart. Probably because they came into the world at a time when children received new levels of attention and educational reform became a priority, they may be the smartest generation yet. Since being smart is part of the Millennial personality, it has been elevated to cool status among this group. Strauss and Howe report that "[d]uring the 1990s, aptitude test scores have risen within every racial and ethnic group, especially in elementary schools. Eight in ten teenagers say it's 'cool to be smart,' while a record share of teenagers say they 'look forward to school,' take advanced placement tests, and plan to attend college."[90]

This outlook has substantial implications, most quite positive, for their worklife. In fact, Claire Raines, author of *Connecting Generations: The Sourcebook*, defines the main components of Millennials' work ethic as revolving around this particularly psychography; in discussing their confidence and optimism, Ms. Raines comments "[r]aised by parents believing in the importance of self-esteem, they characteristically consider themselves ready to overcome challenges and leap tall buildings. Managers who

---

[90] Neil Howe and William Strauss, *Millennials Go to College*, (LifeCourse Associates, 2003).

believe in 'paying your dues' and coworkers who don't think opinions are worth listening to unless they come from someone with a prerequisite number of years on the resume find this can-do attitude unsettling. ... They're described as optimistic yet practical. They believe in the future and their role in it. They've read about businesses with basketball courts, stockrooms stocked with beer for employers, and companies that pay your way through school. They expect a workplace that is challenging, collaborative, creative, fun, and financially rewarding."[91]

> *"I believe that this generation is very confident and feels they can accomplish anything they set their minds to. They are choosy about employer and seem to want an organization that offers challenges, decent pay and adequate time off. We spend more time 'convincing' college recruits that they are wanted. We work closer to them to give them feedback and to understand what they need from us."*
> Sarah Olson, Director of Recruiting
> Berry, Dunn, McNeil & Parker, CPA

The bottom line...Millennials are special, and they have been told all of their lives just how special they are. They had activities planned for them, their schedules were a family priority, and their every success was praised and rewarded. They have earned trophies and awards for participating – not winning, but participating – in a myriad of activities. They have actually been at the forefront of not just the familial agenda, but the societal agenda as well. "During the past decade, in sharp contrast to America's indifference to kids during the Gen-X childhood era, child issues have risen to the top of the nation's political agenda. Youth advocacy groups have multiplied. An entire social marketing industry has risen up to persuade kids to behave better. Social programs for kids remain the one area of government that attracts interest and zeal. Books and magazines for kids, songs for kids, movies for kids, TV and radio programming for kids, web sites for kids – *anything and everything for kids* – have been the hottest media growth markets of the '90s."[92] Okay, so Sesame Street was

---

[91] Claire Raines, "Managing Millennials," *Generations at Work: The Online Home of Claire Raines*, 2002 [http://www.generationsatwork.com/articles/millenials.htm#Millennial%20Characteristics].

[92] Neil Howe and William Strauss, *Millennials Rising: The Next Great Generation* (New York: Vintage Books, 2000).

launched in the year of my birth – 1969 – and there were certainly other child-focused programs and media as I was growing up as a Gen X-er, but there wasn't anything like the attention that Millennials received. One of my favorite examples that comes to mind, for its sheer entertainment value, is Ronald Reagan and the ketchup. Follow my train of thought here... In 1981, just after Reagan took office, Congress cut $1 billion from child-nutrition funding and the USDA had only days to define new standards for school lunches – the idea was that school districts would find ways to economize without compromising nutrition. As part of this process, the USDA put together a panel of nutritionists and food service directors who considered, among other options, defining ketchup as a requisite vegetable when used as an ingredient in recipes and/or as an available condiment (by the way, relish was "on the table" as well – no pun intended there). You have to understand that at that time the USDA standards required that a reimbursable lunch consist of meat, milk, bread, and two servings of fruit or vegetables. Because of the tight 90-day time frame, there wasn't a lot of time for review of the policy recommendations, and they were released (attributed to Reagan's leadership) to some media attention and public scrutiny.[93]

So here's where I draw the contrast: I, and my Gen X peers, were brought up at a time when at least the public perception of government was that it appeared to care so little about kids' needs that they cut funding for subsidized school lunches, a time when language like "latchkey kid" came into the national lexicon. What formal programs and informal colloquialisms came into play in the age of the Millennials? The "No Child Left Behind Act" of 2001, soccer moms, "it takes a village," and "My Kid Is an Honors Student" bumper stickers. Lest I sound bitter or resentful about this shifting societal trend (remember, we Gen X-ers are often characterized as whiners and complainers), let me clearly assert that I am not. I believe that there needed to be an increased focus on kids – it was necessary and it was time. My observation is simply that this came with the Millennials and set the stage for more attention to follow. Some of it wonderful and appropriately placed, and some of it may have been too much and thus contributing to their unrealistic expectations.

---

[93] Cecil Adams, "Did the Reagan-Era USDA Really Classify Ketchup As a Vegetable?" *The Straight Dope*, July 16, 2004, 12/28/08 [http://www.straightdope.com/columns/read/2517/did-the-reagan-era-usda-really-classify-ketchup-as-a-vegetable].

Let's talk about the problematic stuff – I think it is infinitely more interesting. A few years ago, that great research journal *People Magazine* published what I thought was a fascinating article about schools rewarding positive student behavior. The article was entitled "A Gold Star for Good Attendance? No. A New Car!" and had a caption that read "Mustangs, iPods, and laptops – schools are rolling out the perks to get students to get students to show up and earn high marks. But are they teaching the right lesson?" It went on to highlight a few communities, though not the only ones out there, where the schools were rewarding students' good grades and attendance with raffle tickets to win various items. We aren't talking pencil cases and brand new "Trapper Keepers®" here; these kids had the chance to win iPods, laptops, and even cars. Communities rallied together, with local businesses donating goods, to provide the prizes. This is a perfect example of systemic attention, at the local community level, on supporting young people in achieving success. For the record, I don't think this is the decline of society as we know it; I don't see it as a tragedy or a travesty, but I maintain that there is some strong messaging being communicated and internalized with stuff like this. Students are being rewarded, or at least provided with the chance to win rewards, for basically just doing their job – going to school, being on to time class, trying to earn good grades, etc.

There are lots of places where these rewards and celebrations proliferate. Hasn't Little League, and lots of organizations like it, made the transition over the past couple of decades to giving a trophy to every kid, not for winning but basically for showing up? "'They have climbed Mount Everest. They've been down to Machu Picchu to help excavate it. But they've never punched a time clock. They have no idea what it's like to actually be in an office at nine o'clock, with people handing them work,' [Mary] Crane says. She maintains that while this generation has extraordinary technical skills, childhoods filled with trophies and adulation didn't prepare them for the cold realities of work. 'You now have a generation coming into the workplace that has grown up with the expectation that they will automatically win, and they'll always be rewarded, even for just showing up,' Crane says."[94]

---

[94] *60 Minutes* (story synopsis), "The 'Millennials' Are Coming: Morley Safer On The New Generation Of American Workers," May 25, 2007, 10/22/08 [http://www.cbsnews.com/stories/2007/11/08/60minutes/main3475200.shtml#ccmm].

*"What I see is that the Millennials have been raised to think they are special. They have amazing resumes filled with great experiences such as back packing through China, bike riding through Hawaii and writing a travel guide about it, etc. What they don't have is a clear sense that they will have to work to get the job they want. They believe that if they want it, they should have it."*
Susan Kennedy
Job Coach, Career Treking

My colleague Michele told me a story recently about the end-of-season awards event of her young son's soccer team. Eliot, her six-year-old, played on a soccer team this year, and at the end of the season they had a special party, where – yes – every kid got a trophy. Beyond that (and mind you that I do think this is very nice), as the coach presented the trophy to each kid, he made some special remarks about the child. So Eliot got to hear, as his trophy was presented to him, that he was getting it because he scored two goals in the last game. Very exciting for him! One of his friends (let's call him Todd) had his trophy presented to him with the comment that it was for playing in every game. He was devastated. And his parents were devastated for him. And they spoke to the coach afterward about how sad and demoralized Todd was because his reason for getting the trophy wasn't as important as the other children's reasons. So it seems that a trophy for each kid is not enough; every child (and their parent) needs to receive sufficiently valuable and gratifying commentary to go with it.

It is important to caution, once again, that this is not the experience of all Millennials; not every family has the resources to provide their children with these kinds of experiences, not just the trips, treks, and archeological digs, but many children do not even have access to Little League or afterschool soccer. It is marginalizing to forget about those not of the middle or upper class in our society; nonetheless, this theme is quite prevalent and impactful.

*"In the last two organizations I worked for, Millennial workers do demand frequent and positive feedback even when their work is not meeting expectations. They need praise for just showing up or putting forth what they consider to be an effort. They don't seem to understand outcomes and results are what their older supervisors or bosses are concerned about. Millennial workers seem to feel they deserve raises, promotions and bonuses when they work beyond their 8 hours a day, when they choose not to take a lunch or a break. They often feel they deserve a lunch and two 15 minute breaks throughout the day and if they don't take those, the organization owes them something. At both organizations there is tension between Millennial workers and older workers. The expectations are different. Older workers have a stronger work ethic, don't mind putting in their time and overtime and are more committed to the work and the organization. Millennial workers seem to have the attitude that they are only there for a short time and they should be rewarded for just showing up. At Goodwill, there was an effort by HR to design more and more award programs as each year the organizational morale surveys and exit interviews showed that staff wanted to be appreciated more for their work. Much of that feedback came from staff aged 18-26. Goodwill implemented formal awards programs for years with the organization, a peer selected worker of the year award, birthday lunches and referring staff for jobs programs. I did not find they really changed the perspectives of the workers however. They seemed to like to complain."*

Sharon Zimmerman
Deputy Director, WAND (Women's Action for New Directions)
(formerly Vice President for Programs and Services, Goodwill Industries)

Clearly there is some sense of entitlement here, around what Millennials new to the workplace expect from their employers with regard to responsibility, money, and accolades, and I believe that this is a direct consequence of all of the attention and commemoration throughout their childhood.

*"Millennials are a lot more demanding. [They are h]arder to satisfy. Traditional 20-somethings have to pay their dues, start at the bottom, do grunt work.*

*Millennials [are] smart, good with tech[nology], [and] believe they can make meaningful contributions right away. [They w]ant to be taken seriously right away. [They w]ant to be at the table at important meetings. [They want i]mportant assignments. It's not that other gens didn't want it, Millennials [were the] first to ask for it.*

*[They are n]ot afraid to speak to their bosses. They want a lot of responsibilities. They are used to authority. They want to be in charge of projects, and be able to ask for help from the boss.*

*Companies are doing managerial training geared towards [M]illennial employees. Millennials are a huge generation – 75 million in [the] US alone. With upcoming baby boomer retirement, Millennials will have to step into leadership positions a lot earlier than past generations. Millennials will go to the company that will help them acquire the most valuable skills. [They w]atched [their] parents get laid off – Millennials don't believe in corporate loyalty. Organizations are trying to implement policy to convince employees to stay longer. If you don't do what you say, students will leave and tell their friends how crappy your place of employment is."*

Alexandra Levitt

Author, *How'd You Score That Gig*, Millennial Workplace Consultant

It goes back to messaging; more than with any other generation in history, the media has discussed the wide and varied achievements of Millennials, citing almost unbelievable stories of community service performed by even the very youngest of children. As a result, they have seen evidence all of their lives as to how talented and successful they are, and the expectation has been built that they will continue excelling in whatever path they choose for themselves. They place a high premium on this success and have great drive to achieve...and they do work hard to accomplish their goals, be them personal or organizational objectives. And it is extremely important that the content of their work reflects their perceived abilities.

> *"Yes, I believe that Millennials are special. In our organization they have been a jolt of positive energy and garnered lots of positive attention. I also believe that praise motivates Millennials more than other demographic groups. They frame their work in ways that contribute to the world and garners them attention. The group is goal driven. ... They have a hard time with the waiting period between projects, and understanding why they aren't as productive as they once were. ... The group does not know how to work when things are slow. Further, our Millennials have a real hard time with what they view as routine repetitive tasks. If part of their role requires them to generate a weekly report, they will do so for the first several weeks, and then delegate the assignment if they have someone reporting to them, or challenge their manager on the value of the report. It feels like they believe they have so much knowledge and energy that working on routine mundane assignments is a waste."*
>
> Seth Nable, Manager Training and Development
> Human Resources OnProcess Technology

An interesting paradox has been developing. Millennials, as a result of all the praise and adulation, have what is considered by some (especially those older than they) to have an inflated sense of self, a hubris. All of these messages of how wonderful and perfect they are have been internalized, and now they have all this great self-esteem that often leads them to have extraordinarily high – and unreasonable – expectations for their professional lives and to consequently feel underappreciated by their bosses and managers. And we perpetuate this with how we message to them about their important in the workplace.

> *"We have titled flyers at times to stress the 'special issue' - example 'a special job requires a special person'."*
>
> Dan Dern, Assistant Hiring Manager
> YAI / National Institute for People with Disabilities Network

On the other hand, and this other hand is pretty important, they are not stupid and they get that not every trophy means that they actually were the best little soccer player on the team. They grew up seeing that all the other soccer players got trophies too, so the praise and accolades are suspect and only feeds the need for more and more stroking and rewards to validate them. "Despite their confidence and intelligence, Millennials still need more mentoring and personal attention than prior generations. Without lots of projects, Millennials will experience boredom,"[95] states Kip Harrell, author of the online article "Millennials: Your Next Generation Workforce." Mr. Harrell goes on to recommend "eliminat[ing] nebulous time references. 'Pay your dues' and 'two years before your next promotion' will not resonate well with this generation. Focus on end results and productivity with less emphasis on rules on process. Don't squash their ambition. Millennials deserve your attention and your investment in their success. Their parents told them they would be successful, and they will be. Most importantly of all: Embrace them. They are our future, and they're here."[96]

> *"I do find that workers in my organization need more praise and feedback. They also seem to put forth less effort than those of a different generation, and feel that they 'deserve' a good job/ internship while in college. I think this comes from the 'ideal' situations that students think they will be in once they are in or have completed college. Many students feel that since they are in college or about to complete college that they will be making a lot of money in a prestigious career. Our organization raised its intern pay [by] a few more dollars an hour to compensate for the competitive internship market. We also offer college credit and with our positions come priceless sales experience."*
>
> Ashley Humphrey
> Director of Internship Program
> ExamOne, a Quest Diagnostics subsidiary

Not all agree that the issue is that of a more unreasonable need for praise than other generations, though there are some implications for a heightened need for feedback in general, and with greater frequency.

---

[95] Kip Harrell, "Millennials: Your Next Generation Workforce," *Thunderbird School of Global Management Knowledge Network: Research and Opinions*, September 3, 2008 [http://knowledgenetwork.thunderbird.edu/research/2008/09/03/ millennials-%E2%80%93-your-next-generation-workforce/].

[96] Ibid.

*"I am not so sure Millennials are looking for any more praise (than) any new employee no matter what the age; however, they definitely seem more comfortable seeking out feedback for their work. What I have experienced with the Millennials in our office is that they seek out feedback during the process, before completion; almost seems at times looking for someone to give them answers or to tell them how to do something they should know or know how to find. It is easier for them to ask someone then to seek information on their own at times. This seems to manifest in general questions to supervisors and forwarding a presentation asking for suggestions on how to make it better, not taking full ownership until all information is correct."*

Anonymous
HR/Professional Development, Financial Service Industry

In point of fact, some of what we are seeing, possibly as a result of our societal self-esteem movement, is a sense of entitlement that has ugly implications for work life and personal life. Dr. Madeline Levine writes, "[i]n spite of refrigerator doors covered in badges and ribbons, and gold stars awarded for even the slightest effort, kids today are not only not better adjusted than they were thirty or forty years ago, they are actually more emotionally troubled and less academically successful by most measures."[97] While Dr. Levine of course does not advocate for the absence of praise or encouragement in child-rearing, and in fact talks about the great value of it in conveying parental interest, support, appreciation, and warmth, she goes on to discuss what I think is the core of this issue: "[c]hildren need a realistic sense of self, not an inflated sense of self. Indiscriminate praise makes it hard for children to evaluate themselves realistically."[98]

It's not just the rewards that perpetuate these issues; it is also the protection. One of the key issues here, in my opinion, is parental intervention. There is a lot to say about this, and I discussed it much further in the chapter "The Hovered Generation?," but intervening parents have had a great deal to do with the sense of entitlement that is so strongly seen

---

[97] Madeline Levine, Ph.D., *The Price of Privilege: How Parental Pressure and Material Advantage Are Creating a Generation of Disconnected and Unhappy Kids* (New York: HarperCollins Publishers, 2006).

[98] Ibid.

as characterizing Millennials by those who teach, supervise, and work with them. Let's go back to Todd again, and the insufficient remarks from his soccer coach. His parents are like so many others, trying to protect their children from disappointment and unhappiness, stepping in to "fix" things. They speak to coaches making sure their kids get playing time, they talk to teachers about mediocre grades, citing just how hard Johnny worked and thus doesn't he deserve a better grade, and they even talk to bosses about promotions and raises. "Where does this superiority complex come from? If you are looking to attach blame, there's plenty to go around. Blame it on the parents who tell their children every day that they deserve the best and then give it to them. Or the school system that restructures the grading scale by removing 'F' as a failing grade and replacing it with 'Deferred Achievement' so as not to damage the psyches of their substandard students. Or grade school teachers who bend over backward to instill self-esteem with games like The Magic Circle, in which one child wears an 'I'm great' button while all the other kids bury him or her with undeserved compliments. Point the finger at college professors who hand out A's for C- work to avoid confrontation with parents. Or the Internet and cell phone technology that provides instant access and gratification 24/7."[99]

*"I found that they are a very collegial group of people, despite our 10-15 year age differences. They are/were very easy to befriend. As a supervisor, however, I found that they had a great sense of entitlement in terms of the "perks" of their job. If a car home for working after 8 pm was offered, many worked until 8:01 and then had the car take them to a party, or they took a non-employee friend along and dropped them off at another location. We also had many incidents of signing-in, then going to the gym, then coming back to work, with the entire day "billed". Generally, for offenses like these, they would be called in, and slapped on the wrist, as they say. Unfortunately, this age group seems to try to get a lot of explanations of the reasons why these things are not legitimate, and argues their case very thoroughly. There doesn't seem to be an understanding of "because the rules say you can't do it. Wide spread abuse would cost the firm a lot of money and insurance issues."* (cont. on page 130)

---

[99] D.A. Hayden and Michael Wilder, *From B.A. to Payday: Launching Your Career After College* (New York: Stewart, Tabori, & Chang: 2008).

> *(cont. from page 129)*
> *"It seems that they were always negotiating. They seem not to be very judgmental, they are open-minded socially, politically, intellectually, but this seem to make them insist that all things are open to negotiation."*
> Anonymous
> Manager of paralegals, various New York law firms

What I fear has been instilled is a warped sense of expectation and definition of fairness. We often hear disappointment being reflected back as "it's not fair." The countless conversations I have had with students, and their parents, for that matter, just on what I see as the fairly insignificant issue of a class for which they want to register filling up before they get a shot at it. First of all, the drama that this seems to engender; you would think it is the end of the world...again, for the parents as much as the students. Secondly, the discussion always ultimately devolves to "but I wanted it." This notion of wanting something translating to it being yours to have no matter what completely eludes me, yet it seems to exist in the Millennial mindset quite vibrantly. And there seems to be no getting past "it's not fair."

> *"It seems for us that this generation requires more recognition than others seem to need. We have found that this generation wants to be promoted every six months or feel they deserve it rather then that they have earned it. We developed more formal job descriptions and are working on developing more clear-cut progression paths."*
> Anonymous
> HR Business Partner, Multimedia Publishing Company

Clearly, this is not simply a parental issue, but one of societal conditioning, and thus comes with some significant implications. "The professors [Barbara Keats and Dale Kalika of the W.P. Carey School of Business] also advise bosses to be mindful of the Millennials' need for praise. Remember, this peer group grew up in an age when every kid on the team was a star, regardless of how many strikes against them. ... The result, the professor[s] say, is that these young people crave approval and respond best to what Kalika calls 'persuasive means. Be a facilitator, a mentor, not just an authority.' Remember, too, that the 'sandwich' trick of sticking criticism between two compliments might not work. Keats points to 'the serial position effect,' a phenomenon named by researchers who found that people tend to remember beginnings and endings of lists, not middles. Kalika explains: 'If I say, 'Barbara, you're doing very well in A, B and C. There are, however, some areas where I want you to improve: D and E. Nevertheless, you're really good in A, B and C.' That D and E become discounted.'"[100]

Another interesting element is the validation that social media provides, which I believe lends itself to an exaggerated sense of self-importance. Millennials are constantly posting the status of their activities to their Facebook sites and instant messaging profiles. And they have an audience for it. Their friends and family – and even strangers – seem to want to know what they are doing or thinking at any given moment. This gets internalized over time, and conveys to them that all that they do is of prime importance – not just to them, but to most anyone around them. The other day I observed some podcasts available on I-Tunes, and I downloaded a couple of them that piqued my curiosity. In one, a young woman broadcasts her lengthy opinions and interpretations of her favorite TV shows. Several of her podcasts are more than an hour in length. She was, in my opinion, terribly inarticulate and uninspired. But she goes on making these recordings, and posting them to I-Tunes, where I assume they must have at least a meager audience. Just like blogging. Admittedly, I watch a fair amount of television, and have been known to engage in my share of "water cooler chats" about the exciting turn of events on the previous night's episode of *Lost*, but I could never imagine that anyone outside of a small circle of friends and co-workers are really interested in my analysis, and even some of them are just tolerating it because they are nice people. I think that the ability to post, whether in a blog or a podcast, one's every thoughts and reactions reinforces some idea that everything you say is important and interesting to others. This contributes to this sense of self-importance and narcissism.

---

[100] Knowledge@W.P.Carey, "Millennials in the Workplace: R U Ready?" March 26, 2008, 12/29/08 [http://knowledge.wpcarey.asu.edu/article.cfm?articleid=1580].

*"Yes. I think that Millennials have a strong urge for validation, and I can't help but wonder if this is an after effect of the development of Web 2.0 and social media like Facebook. During previous generations, validation largely came from a relatively small group of one's peers. However, with the development of social media, validation can come from countless scores of one's 'friends.' It's a new kind of peer pressure: social media sites like Facebook and Twitter constantly invite you to share what you're doing . . . and invite your 'friends' to comment on it. The end result is a group of individuals who both (a) take as a given that all of their 'friends' actually care what they are doing, and, (b) need their cohort to validate those activities by commenting on them.*

*"This need for validation works its way into the workplace. This past summer, I hired a student fresh out of college to perform some information technology-related tasks. The tasks are fairly repetitive in nature, and I regularly assign them, send the individual on his/her way, and await their return upon completion. Some assumptions have to be made about how to perform the work, and, on the whole, these assumptions are made and performed accurately. This summer, however, our summer recruit had a consistent need for validation. 'Is this how you want the computer set up?' 'Do you want me to <insert terribly obvious next step to perform here>?' 'Should I move on to <insert self-evident next task here>?'"*

R. Kyle Jones
President, EduSophia

One big question here, of course, is will this entitlement change as the current economy impacts their career options and trajectory. All of the sudden, they have been slapped in the face with the fact that no matter how special they think they are, no matter how wonderful they have been told they are, what they want isn't "a birthright." There is no getting around the fact that times are tough, and "but I worked so hard" doesn't translate into the job of their dreams...or even a job at all. Look, it's hard to know at this relatively early point how this will affect their psychology and overall outlook, but there are some early indicators that it has sunk in a bit. "Jessica Buchsbaum first noticed that something had changed in May 2008. The head of recruitment for a law firm in Florida, Ms. Buchsbaum was used to interviewing young candidates for summer internships who seemed to think that the world owed them a living. Many applicants expected the firm to promote itself to them rather than the other way around. However, last May's crop was far more humble. 'The tone had changed from 'What can you do for me?' to 'Here's what I can do for you', she says."[101] Despite these realizations about a new reality, Millennials may still be finding it hard to shift their expectations about how the workplace demonstrates its valuing of them. "Because of the downturn, Net Geners are finding it harder to hop to new jobs. At the same time, their dissatisfaction is growing as crisis-hit firms adopt more of a command-and-control approach to management – the antithesis of the open, collaborative style that young workers prefer. Less autonomy and more directives have sparked complaints among Net Geners that offices and factories have become 'pressure cookers' and 'boiler rooms'. 'The recession is creating lower turnover, but also higher frustration among young people stuck in jobs,' warns Cam Marston, a consultant who advises companies on inter-generational matters."[102] Despite difficult economic times, Millennials still perceive themselves as having lots of professional options, and companies will continue to find themselves "selling" the job to prospective young employees.

*"I believe that this generation is very confident and feels they can accomplish anything they set their minds to. They are choosy about employers and seem to want an organization that offers challenges, decent pay and adequate time off. We spend more time 'convincing' college recruits that they are wanted. We work closer to them to give them feedback and to understand what they need from us."*
Sarah Olson
Director of Recruiting, Berry, Dunn, McNeil & Parker, CPA

Aaron Green, Founder and President of Professional Staffing Group and PSG Offshore Resources, and a member of the Board of Directors of the American Staffing Association, suggests that Millennials' high expectations for their own career advancement will not be subjugated, as they continue to scout for increasingly interesting and gratifying work. "[T]hey've got reason to feel this way – with Baby Boomers retiring and fewer workers to replace them in Gen X, demographics point to a sustained demand for Gen

---

[101] "Generation Y Goes to Work," *The Economist*, January 3, 2009.

[102] Ibid.

Y workers. Furthermore, so far this recession has seen a disproportionate number of job cuts among senior workers, with heftier salaries and benefits, as compared with relatively lower-paid, less experienced workers."[103] Green suggests that as long as this is mitigated by logical and long-term planning, Millennials can – and do – expect the same professional rewards that they have always had.

It will be hard for Millennials to get past their roots and conditioning; they have been raised in a culture that tells them how wonderful and deserving of success that they are, and consequently they have extremely high expectations for themselves, and they hold others to the same standards. As a result, there is clearly a careful balance of praise and criticism that needs to be managed with them as adults. "Thanks to over-involved [B]oomer parents, this cohort has been coddled and pumped up to believe they can achieve anything. ... Cindy Pruitt, a professional development and recruiting manager with the national law firm Womble Carlyle Sandridge & Rice, shares with disbelief a recent incident in which one of the firm's summer associates broke down in her office after being told his structure on a recent memo was 'a little too loose.' 'They're simply stunned when they get any kind of negative feedback,' Pruitt says. 'I practically had to walk him off the ledge.'"[104] Millennials have grown up amidst a sea of exaltation and glorification that have been a near-constant theme. **So what do we do?** How do we as organizations manage the supervision of adult employees who have such a strong need for feedback and also have an inflated sense of self, and the expectations for reward that accompanies it?

- **Feedback is key.**

This is certainly not a new concept, but has become increasingly important with the Millennial generation. Millennials are accustomed to receiving substantial feedback and are actually quite solicitous of it. It is a shift of business practices for many organizations to provide feedback and evaluation with the level of frequency that Millennials desire and to which they respond. Many organizations are developing more regular evaluation cycles, while additionally assessing the ways in which they deliver criticism.

---

[103] Aaron Green, "How the Recession Impacts Job Outlook for the Millennials," *The Boston Globe HR Center On Staffing*, December 15, 2008 [http://www.boston.com/jobs/employers/hr/hrcolumns/2008/12/how_the_recession_impacts_job.html].

[104] Danielle Sacks, "Scenes from the Culture Clash," *Fast Company*, January 2006.

*"Luckily with Kelly Services, constant feedback is a commitment to our ongoing quality management process. For sixty years the same tool has been effective in measuring performance. For us we are able, not only to measure the quality of what we do here, but the quality of our employees. Our vision is to be the world's best staffing services solutions provider. To do that, we implore each employee to look for ways to improve. We do that by monthly quantitative analysis of four core areas: quality of work performed, quantity of work performed, attendance and punctuality and interpersonal skills. That being said, that only answers half of the question. No, we have not changed the way that we measure our employees; however the feedback delivery has changed a bit. One of the things that I have noticed in the past few years is that although they require more constant feedback, they perceive that these reviews are always positive; the employees will hear only what they want to hear. We deliver our messages rather strategically, offering highlights and areas of success, followed by areas for improvement. However, I see that employees cling to and understand the highlights, but almost do not hear the negatives. If they do hear the negatives, often our time is spent dealing with their defensiveness.*

*"We have a long history of providing skill development and training. Although, it is difficult to get these employees to spend time on their career development and 'hard skills.' What I see is that they believe that on-the-job training is enough. What they do not realize is that the workforce is competitive and requires more than the basics to get the job done."*

Cynthia Levinson
On-Site Supervisor at State Street Corporation, Kelly Complete

The feedback mechanisms don't always have to be formal and structured. First of all, I don't believe that it is our responsibility to overhaul all of our protocols to meet this overdeveloped need in the generation. Part of their adjustment process is learning to cope with what we all-too-often refer to as "the real world." And they can.

*"When it changed for me was when I went to college. I grew up in a small town and then went off to a very large university. I was in a classroom with anywhere from 30-500 students, with the average class size being around 250. When I wrote a paper that I thought was exceptional, I rarely got feedback from a professor. Even when I took an exam, I got a letter grade, but no comments in the margins telling me what I did right or wrong, like I was used to from my high school teachers. My parents no longer rewarded me for a good grade because that was what was expected of a college student. I started getting accustomed to less feedback and fewer rewards, which I feel better prepared me for my post-college life. Now that I have a career I know that there are going to be many days where I hear very little feedback from my boss on how I'm doing. Although I still enjoy hearing my boss praise me or even tell me where I could improve, I no longer expect this. It is hard not being recognized when I feel like I went over and beyond, but I've learned that that's life."*

Faryn Rosen (Millennial)
Talent Acquisition Specialist, HR OnProcess Technology

We must remember that what is most important to Millennials is that they get the guidance and indicators regarding their work, not that it is in a formal setting and documented in writing. And what is most important to us is that it is delivered in a manner that they can "hear" it.

*"In my organization, these workers seek feedback more readily. They need continual reassurance about their work product. They expect the feedback to be balanced. As a result, we in management have started using the "sandwich technique" praise-criticism-praise. We've found that these workers take criticism personally and are slow to recover from a misstep. In my work experience in the past, managers would only call you into their office if something was wrong."*

Anonymous
Assistant Director, Career Development Non-Profit Organization

*"I absolutely believe that they need to be developed with coping. While they are excellent in follow up, they are hard to accept constructive criticism at work. I think that performance management through the year is an important balance for the [M]illennials."*
Maren Mercado
HR Generalist, McGladrey & Pullenn

There certainly can be great value to enhancing how we supervise our employees of any age, providing more mentorship and direction than have been the trend of the past. As well, through productive group meetings where everyone checks in about the progress on their various projects, it provides an avenue for feedback from peers – something that Millennials find of great value – as well as affords opportunities for idea-sharing.

*"We have taken some steps to improve communication and provide better guidance and employee relations. My focus has been with our entry level Millennials by the following:*

*• MONTHLY PROGRESS MEETINGS. These meetings are done individually, in a casual environment. Here we discuss their progress as well as any issues they may have.*

*• WEEKLY GROUP MEETINGS – Weekly meetings provide a 'catch up' for the week and to see what is coming up the next week. It also allows time for us to receive feedback as well as possible solutions from the group, looking to them to help us find solutions. The weekly meetings also provide us an opportunity to provide some professional development in discussions anywhere from phone etiquette to proper dress. What we have found in having these meetings with an open forum for discussion is that the Millennials are aware they have much to learn as many have never worked in a corporate environment, so proper attire and basic office procedures are new to them. What I have taken away from our Millennials thus far is that, even what I may think is a 'no brainer' some Millennials have no idea!"*
Anonymous
HR/Professional Development, Financial Service Industry

- **Coaching programs work.**

Coaching is another tremendous way to provide formal feedback to Millennials, but from a source that is not a manager or supervisor. Remember, many Millennials have been raised with a plethora of "coaches" in one form or another (sports, afterschool activities, tutors), and they are quite accustomed to the attention that comes with it. Work-based mentoring and coaching programs allow more seasoned professionals to facilitate the professional growth process of newer employees and give them necessary evaluation of their workplace contributions in a non-threatening manner, thus potentially enabling their openness to actually hearing messages that they might otherwise debate with their manager.

> *"I do believe that this generation wants more feedback. We have implemented a weekly 30-minute coaching session to offer feedback and answer questions as well as provide a weekly focus."*
> Ed Ayala
> Vice President, Strategies for Wealth
>
> *"Millennials were taught to express themselves and receive reward for hard work. We have a mentor and buddy program that assists with them in receiving important feedback on their internship."*
> Maren Mercado
> HR Generalist, McGladrey & Pullen

A more seasoned colleague who serves as an assigned organizational coach can help introduce the new employee to the institutional culture, and when needed – provide a reality check about how best to conduct oneself professionally. It is also another way to help bridge the proverbial "generation gap," as it allows the Boomers and Gen X-ers to develop a new understanding and appreciation of their new colleagues, and can even have positive implications for product or service development.

> *"[A n]ew Hallmark program to bridge generational gaps: A CURRENT creative division-sponsored exercise pairs employees from different generations and encourages them to discuss differences or similarities they see between one another's generations. The exercises are intended to build empathy between generations working at Hallmark and also to build an understanding of what consumers of different generations relate to and want."*
> *(cont. on page 139)*

*(cont. from page 138)*
*"At Hallmark, increasing empathy among generations can provide valuable insights as we develop products, merchandising and marketing."*
Julie Wille
College Recruiting Representative, Hallmark Cards

Some companies are even moving to tech-based peer feedback programs, reports *The Economist* magazine. "The creators of a new, web-based service called Rypple claim that it can satisfy Net Geners' desire for frequent assessments while easing the burden on their supervisors. The service requires employees to establish a network of trusted peers, mentors and managers whose opinions they value. They can then send out short questions, such as 'What did you think of my presentation today?', to which their network's members can respond online. The responses are kept anonymous so that, at least in theory, employees cannot tell who has made them."[105] For a generation that is characterized not only by their need for constant feedback, but also by their technological orientation, programs like these are sure to be a hit.

- **Recognition of what Millennials bring.**
At their core, like any employee, Millennials want to feel valued by their organization. This is the "celebration" that they seek now that they are in the workplace. There are many ways to do this, most certainly including the obvious formal award. While I am reluctant about it, there is something to the notion of ceremonial recognition of contribution. I am frustrated by the fact that our society has become so conditioned around this that any lack of award or accolade is an affront, but the fact is that this is true. I often remind students, employees, and even myself that the reward for doing our job is called "a paycheck," but one cannot deny the sway within any organization of receiving an official honor for a "job well done."

---

[105] The RyppleEffect," *The Economist*, January 3, 2009.

> *"What Kelly has done, in our market, is re-introduced a comprehensive employee recognition program. We have seen that this generation thrives on competition; we give employees a reward for going 'above and beyond.' This recognition of peers sets the bar for healthy competition and the motivation for the reward seems to beat out the message that any job worth doing is worth doing well."*
>
> Cynthia Levinson
> On-Site Supervisor at State Street Corporation, Kelly Complete

Equally, if not more importantly, is the recognition that comes with being given extra responsibility at work that conveys trust and appreciation. After all, as conditioned for praise as they are, Millennials have been through the whole "everybody gets a trophy" thing, and they have grown skeptical of it. This is to some extent too obvious, and what is really of benefit is the assignment of interesting work versus what Millennials deem as "grunt work." This generation has a hard time understanding that not every assignment is going to be ground breaking and exciting, as D.A. Hayden and Michael Wilder address in their "advice" book for job-seeking Millennials. "Ask students to describe the type of job they're seeking, and some start with a list of all the things they don't want in a job. ... Maybe we're old-fashioned, but almost every one of the jobs we've held over the years involves some of all of these 'don'ts.' But mixed in among all that drudgery were some pretty exciting and rewarding moments that made it all worthwhile. Every job, however glamorous it appears to you from the outside, has its boring moments. So be aware that when you rattle off your list of exclusions and qualifications, what you are really saying to your interviewer is 'I'm too smart and well educated to waste my time doing menial stuff. You need to find important things for me to do.'"[106] This advice is pretty obvious to most of us in the older generations, but is not necessarily so for your average Millennial. And the fact that they are so eager for meaningful projects at work is clearly an advantage. Particularly important for when the economy improves is keeping the Millennials intellectually engaged now: "[y]ounger workers will have to accept that in difficult times decisions will be taken more crisply and workloads will increase. Their managers, meanwhile, will have to make an extra effort to keep Net Geners engaged and motivated. Firms that cannot pull off this balancing

---

[106] D.A. Hayden and Michael Wilder, *From B.A. to Payday: Launching Your Career After College* (New York: Stewart, Tabori, & Chang: 2008).

act could see an exodus of young talent once the economy improves."[107] A savvy manager can disperse more interesting projects to reward a talented and hard-working employee. This, more than praise, is a clear indicator of their value. After all, they have experienced a childhood of praise being doled out to them almost indiscriminately (remember every little leaguer getting a trophy), and this has led to some questioning of its validity.

*"The needs of the Millennial Generation are definitely different than the needs of generations in the past. I do not however feel that it is the praise and reward they really seek. Not saying it doesn't matter; I just don't think that is the main thing that drives them. What makes the Millennials tick in my opinion is the reassurance that what they are doing matters and that they themselves matter. The Millennials wants to know that they belong. They want to feel that they are needed."*
Bill Phillips
Sr. Recruiting Specialist
(Strategic Talent Development)
Duke Energy Corporation

*"Being a [M]illennial myself, I have to agree with this [Do you find that Millennial workers in your organization express more need than other generations for feedback and expect frequent praise and rewards for their efforts?]. There is so much pressure and competition to be the best. We are extremely hard on ourselves when we are not the best. Because there is a lot expected out of us, we look to those who can provide comfort and reassurance that we are good hard working people who are in fact making a difference.*

*"My company deals directly with this generation through our internship program and there are quite a few programs in place to recognize their efforts and provide praise and feedback. Our interns have a college unit director who serves as their coach that they can go to for advice."*
Becky Girola
Director of Recruiting, Northwestern Mutual Financial Network

---

[107] "Generation Y Goes to Work," *The Economist*, January 3, 2009.

Hayden and Wilder state, "[f]airly or unfairly, today's crop of college students and recent graduates have been labeled the entitlement generation."[108] I argue that their lifetime of the combination of exaggerated praise, protection from disappointment and disillusion, and the ubiquitous influence of technology on ego has formed a lot of who this generation is and what they expect from all facets of their lives, most notably their work environs. In short, I am quite concerned that while it may be very well-intentioned, all of this celebration of Millennials can and often does go overboard, and that can be both thorny and complicated. The "Celebrated Generation" is here, and we need to understand their impact.

## CHAPTER FIVE: SUMMARY

• There has been a cumulative effect of the outpouring of acknowledgement and reward that Millennials have seen throughout their lives. We have raised a new "celebrated generation" and it has its impact. Much research indicates that Millennials are a generation raised with the expectation of constant praise and accolades. One positive outcome is Millennials' robust sense of self and self-worth that should be appreciated, and perhaps emulated, by other generations.

• Millennials are special, and they have been told all of their lives just how special they are. They had activities planned for them, their schedules were a family priority, and their successes were praised and rewarded. They have earned trophies and awards for simply participating in their myriad of activities. And they have been at the forefront of not just the familial agenda, but the societal agenda as well.

• It is now "cool" to be smart, and, probably because they came into the world at a time when children received new levels of attention and educational reform became a priority, Millennials may be the smartest generation yet. This has substantial implications, most quite positive, for their worklife.

*(cont. on page 143)*

---

[108] D.A. Hayden and Michael Wilder, *From B.A. to Payday: Launching Your Career After College* (New York: Stewart, Tabori, & Chang: 2008).

## CHAPTER FIVE: SUMMARY (continued)

- Ironically, despite their confidence and intelligence, Millennials still need more mentoring and personal attention than prior generations.

- Social media may lend itself to an exaggerated sense of self-importance; Millennials are constantly posting the status of their activities to their Facebook sites and instant messaging profiles, with an audience of friends and family – and even strangers – seeming to want to know what they are doing or thinking at any given moment. This gets internalized over time, and conveys to them that all that they do is of prime importance to most anyone around them. This contributes to a sense of self-importance and grandiosity.

- Despite difficult economic times, Millennials may still perceive themselves as having lots of professional options, and companies will continue to find themselves "selling" the job to prospective young employees. Their high expectations for their own career advancement will not be subjugated, as they continue to seek out increasingly interesting and gratifying work.

- As organizations address these Millennial characteristics, they will find it helpful to develop more regular evaluation cycles, while additionally assessing the ways in which criticism is delivered. Formal coaching programs can be a useful tool, whereby more seasoned professionals serve as a resource to newer Millennial employees, but recognition of the skills sets and talents that Millennials bring to the workplace will be essential to their professional satisfaction as well.

# CHAPTER 6

## Millennials - Generation Optimistic?

O n November 9, 2008, just days after what may have been the most historic presidential election of our time, the *New York Times* published "Generation O Gets Its Hopes Up," an article by Damien Cave that gave yet another sobriquet to the oft-renamed Millennial Generation. The "O" to which Mr. Cave refers is of course the new President of the United States, Barack Obama, but he could just as easily be calling them "Generation Optimistic" as "Generation Obama." Cave suggests that the generation may now forever be known as Generation O; I think time will tell with that, but I certainly agree that Obama has captured the hopes and dreams of the up-and-coming youth in a huge way, and represents a vision of the future to a generation who look to government overall, and Barack specifically, to make positive change in the world. There is a lot of information about Millennials that has suggested significant concern amidst the positive, but this is an area which is supremely encouraging.

It is estimated that somewhere between 21 and 24 million voters between the ages of 18 to 29 voted in the 2008 Presidential election – this is up at least 2 million, and possibly as much as almost 4.5 million, from four years prior. According to some exit polls, nearly 70 percent of these young voters went for Obama. This is due in large part to the fact that Obama "gets" the Millennials, and they know it. Take Facebook, for example: in the November 17, 2008 *Online Media Daily* article by Matthew Fraser and Soumitra Dutta, the authors discuss the huge role that Facebook and other social networking sites played in this groundbreaking electoral season. "This election was the first time that all candidates – presidential and congressional – attempted to connect directly with American voters via online social networking sites like Facebook and MySpace. It has even been called the 'Facebook election.' It is no coincidence that one of Obama's key strategists was 24-year-old Chris Hughes, a Facebook co-founder. It was Hughes who masterminded the Obama campaign's highly effective Web blitzkrieg – everything from social networking sites to podcasting and mobile messaging."[109] According to the authors, Obama was savvy enough to not limit himself to the better known networking sites like Facebook; he, like the Generation that may now even carry his name (or at least his initial), tuned into a wide plethora, including YouTube, MySpace, Twitter, Flickr, Digg, BlackPlanet, LinkedIn, AsianAve, MiGente, Glee and others I wouldn't begin to pretend I have even heard of...and in doing so, he connected with Millennials in a way that his rivals – first Hillary Clinton and then John McCain – were unable.

The proof is in the numbers on this one: while McCain could only count approximately 600,000 "friends" on Facebook, Barack's buddies numbered over two million. As of this writing in late November 2008, a YouTube search for Barack Obama channels on YouTube turns up 1,080, while a similar search for John McCain provides 387 links. Now, it should be noted that a general search on YouTube for videos for each of these candidates shows McCain in the lead with 171,000 videos to Obama's 139,000; on the other hand, a search for "Yes We Can Obama" produces 8,690 results, including the 'Yes We Can Barack Obama Music Video' which, from its posting ten months ago, has been viewed an astounding 14,149,623 times. Further, as Fraser and Dutta report, "[o]n the micro-blogging platform Twitter, Obama could count on more than 112,000 supporters 'tweeting' to get him elected. McCain, for his part, had only 4,600 followers on Twitter."[110]

In short, this is a politically active generation, and a lot of their activity does take place online. As Palfrey and Gasser discuss in *Born Digital: Understanding the First Generation of Digital Natives*, "Digital Natives have been at the forefront of the movement to change politics through the use of digital tools."[111] The October 2006 Harvard Institute of Politics (IOP) survey of 18-24 year olds reported that 48 percent said they had signed an online petition, 31 percent had written an email or letter advocating a political position, 29 percent had contributed to an political discussion or blog advocating a political position, 21 percent had attended a politi-

---

[109] Matthew Fraser and Soumitra Dutta, "Obama and the 'Facebook Effect'," *Online Media Daily* November 17, 2008, 11/28/08 [http://www.mediapost.com/publications/?fa=Articles.showArticleHomePage&art_aid=94861].

[110] Ibid.

[111] John Palfrey and Urs Gasser, *Born Digital: Understanding the First Generation of Digital Natives* (New York: Basic Books, 2008).

cal rally, 18 percent had donated money to a political campaign or cause, and 14 percent had volunteered on a political campaign for a candidate or issue. Additionally, 60 percent said they followed news about national politics closely.[112] In a June 2007 report by the New Politics Institute, a political think-tank, this IOP survey is further analyzed, noting that "60 percent [of the 18-24 year-olds surveyed] thought political engagement was an effective way of solving important issues facing the country and 71 percent thought such engagement was an effective way of solving important issues facing their local community. Millennials disagree with the idea that if the federal government runs something, it is necessarily inefficient and wasteful."[113]

The Harvard University 15th Biannual Youth Survey on Politics and Public Service cites "when young Obama voters were asked to describe as thoughtfully as possible the reason that they are supporting the Illinois Senator, 30 percent mentioned, 'can make a change' and 14 percent said 'fresh new voice and perspective' – for a total of 44 percent citing change related themes."[114]

Obviously, it is not just about the numbers—it is really about the message that has garnered this kind of support, including financial. As early as February 17, 2007, Peter Levine, Deputy Director of the Center for Information and Research on Civic Learning and Engagement, a nonpartisan research center at the University of Maryland, was quoted in an article by Jose Antonio Vargas for the *Washington Post* discussing Obama's appeal to today's younger voters: "Obama's message is attractive to a certain type of young person. He's saying: 'You have a role to play. This is about you. About your role.' There's a real hunger for that kind of message."[115] This

---

[112] Harvard University Institute of Politics, "The 11th Biannual Youth Survey on Politics and Public Service," November 1, 2006, 11/28/08 [http://www.iop.harvard.edu/var/ezp_site/storage/fckeditor/file/pdfs/Research-Publications/fall_2006_topline.pdf].

[113] New Politics Institute, "The Progressive Politics of the Millennial Generation," June 20, 2007, 11/28/08 [http://www.newpolitics.net/node/360].

[114] Harvard University Institute of Politics, "The 15th Biannual Youth Survey on Politics and Public Service," October 22, 2008, 11/28/08 [http://www.iop.harvard.edu/Research-Publications/Polling/Fall-2008-Survey].

[115] Jose Antonio Vargas, "Young Voters Find Voice on Facebook," *Washington Post*, February 17, 2007.

has great appeal for a generation that has been raised with such strong messaging about their value and worth for the world around them. The verbatim comments from the young adults surveyed in the Harvard Biannual Youth Survey on Politics and Public Service best exemplify this feeling amongst Millennial voters.

*"He speaks to my generation in a way that no other candidate has and actually addresses the concerns that are specific to us. He represents change and hope in a political climate that is falling apart in a way that speaks to even the most cynical and bitter citizen."* - **18-year-old white male at Oregon State.**

*"He supports progress toward a better global reputation and foreign relations. He supports a health-care system that is on the side of the people, not the corporations. He represents a change in the direction of the nation, toward greater equality for men, women, and minorities."* - **20-year-old white female enrolled at Georgia Tech.**

*He is a dynamic candidate who understands the struggles faced by the poor, middle class, and generally disadvantaged. He is ready to set the nation on a different path than it is heading."* - **20-year-old African American female enrolled at Barnard College.**[116]

This faith in government and optimistic hopes for our new path will be especially important if, as seems likely, we continue with the current economic downturn. Remember, Millennials can be typified by their belief that it is up to them to improve the world from the mess that was made by their predecessors. Obama's inclusionary and consensus-oriented approach has great appeal to a generation that is so used to teaming and groupwork. They are well-documented as trusting of teams and systems – at least until their expectations are not met, at which point there may be hell to pay – and Obama, initially at least, appears to embody the optimism that typifies this younger generation. They seem to believe that Obama's government is one that will value transparency, much like that of Facebook and other social networking sites. I find this faith quite amusing given that he is a Gen X-er himself, a generation that is often held in contempt by our Millennial successors due to their view that Generation X is just a bunch of jaded complainers. Personally, as an X-er myself, I take umbrage with this, but one cannot deny the force of optimism that personify the Millennials.

---

[116] Harvard University Institute of Politics, "The 15th Biannual Youth Survey on Politics and Public Service," October 22, 2008, 11/28/08 [http://www.iop.harvard.edu/Research-Publications/Polling/Fall-2008-Survey].

But will this optimism continue unfazed? Millennials about to graduate from college are facing a tremendously difficult job market, and newly employed Millennials are losing jobs as companies face cutbacks and are forced to downsize. And the parents of these young people are not poised to help out with finances as they may have been in the past. It is a tough situation all around, and time will tell how the Millennials react in the face of this adversity. Past experience suggests that they will be pretty stressed out about it, perhaps creating further anxiety issues, but that they also might rise to the occasion with their internal resources of optimism and determination. The big question is, will a generation that has really mostly seen overall societal prosperity find their perspective on their world quite shaken by this economic downturn? I guess that we will see...past experience also tells us that it may be that they see opportunity for betterment coming from all of this, and that they see themselves at the heart of this change.

So, "Generation O?" These optimists are not just Obama supporters; after all, more than 30 percent are believed to have voted for another candidate for President, so they are not all connected by a common political candidate or ideology. But they may be connected by their optimism and a common desire to make the world a better place. Even amongst business students, who are often stereotyped as only being about the "almighty dollar," there is a revolution happening. In the November 24, 2008 issue of *Business Week Magazine*, Geoff Gloeckler reports in The Millennials Invade the B-Schools, "[s]ure, MBAs are still attracted to investment banks and accounting firms, but students from the Millennial Generation are increasingly interested in jobs where they feel they can make a positive difference – whether that's building solar panels, running a food bank, or making microfinance loans in Africa."[117] Gloeckler goes on to state, "[e]lectives in such areas as sustainability and renewable energy are appearing in more course catalogs. And at Harvard, the Social Enterprise Club has replaced the finance and management clubs as most popular on campus. Carl Kester, finance professor and deputy dean of academic affairs, says that while idealism wasn't altogether absent in the past, it has picked up steam. 'It's become very prominent since the Millennial Generation arrived at our doorstep,' he says."[118]

---

[117] Geoff Gloeckler, "The Millennials Invade the B-Schools," *Business Week*, November 13, 2008.

[118] Ibid.

Business schools are not the only ones who are reacting. Plenty of companies are overhauling their employee recruitment materials to bring attention to their community service and environmental initiatives, all in an effort to attract the interest of prospective Millennial employees.

So the Millennials, with all their optimism and drive, are more focused than ever on doing good. But they also, as the expression goes, want to do **well** by doing good. Don't forget, in their seminal book on the generation, *Millennials Rising: The Next Great Generation*, William Strauss and Neil Howe devote a full chapter to Millennials and consumerism, discussing not just the buying power of this group, but also the consumer-oriented focus of this group. And Strauss and Howe called it on this conclusion way back in 2000 when the book was published: "Millennials are a consumer behemoth, riding atop a new youth economy of astounding scale and extravagance. Plainly, not all kids have shared in the recent prosperity, but tens of millions have – and the aggregate numbers speak for themselves. Purchases by and for children age 4 to 12 tripled over the 1990s, and teens hit their stride at the decade's end. ... What's' behind this explosion? It's come much too fast to be solely the result of the rising number of youths or (even) the growth in youth or adult income. The fact is, everyone is spending more on kids – kids on themselves, parents on their own kids, and nonparents on their young friends and relatives. Many Americans worry that all this spending is spoiling today's youth. But no one can deny that adults are trying to favor this generation by steering more money towards its wants and less toward their own...."[119]

And Millennials have maintained this brand of consumerism with a focus on the big brands – not just in clothes and cars, but also in schools and jobs. The big brand school will get them the high-powered job at the big name company and allow them the success for which they yearn, the success that they have always been told is theirs for the taking. Their upbringing has been one characterized by celebration of accomplishment, trophies for every little leaguer and graduation ceremonies at the end of each year in school. They have received constant messaging about their own value and worth, and it has not only been personalized, but it also appears to be materializing. And with it comes the desire not just for success in the broader sense, but also for the trappings of success. And so they spend.

---

[119] Neil Howe and William Strauss, *Millennials Rising: The Next Great Generation*, (New York: Vintage Books, 2000).

It has been estimated that the Millennial Generation has billions of dollars in purchasing power, though of course this may change in these tough economic times. In fact, just four years ago one in three Millennial teens had a credit card. And, according to a recent *Time Magazine* article, Millennials wield a lot of power not just with their own credit cards but with those of their parents. "Retailers of the world, take note: If you want to get into a boomer's pocketbook, you've got to win her daughter over first. According to Resource Interactive, an Ohio-based marketing company, young adults influence 88% of household apparel purchases."[120]

Companies need to consider the particular buying habits of Millennials. A report from the *Economist Magazine Intelligence Unit* entitled "Maturing with the Millennials: Are Organizations Prepared for the Millennial Consumer?" holds that the generation is far more concerned with peer recommendation and viral marketing (i.e., online promotional communications passed from one customer to another) than they are with corporate reputation, and brand is less important when deciding what they want to buy. Millennial responders to the *Economist's* survey prioritized convenience over price in their purchasing decisions. Further, the report cites that "a sampling of comments point to convenience, customisation, community and 'cool' as motivating factors for millennials. Others include 'fast, reliable service', 'frictionless interaction', a 'tailored approach', 'honesty and trust' and a 'personal touch.'"[121]

Moreover, "this generation is drawn to 'mass brand experiences' which appeal to their communal, pro-social nature, and according to the 2008 College Explorer study, this year's college class (age 18-30) brings with it a record $237 billion in consumer spending, an increase of 20 percent since 2007. It's a ripe field for responsible brands."[122] Since Millennials' buying is more influenced by the Internet than any other media, with exposure to anywhere from 300 to 1,000 online ads daily, virtually all marketers utilize

---

[120] Deirdre Van Dyk, "Who's Holding the Handbag," *Time*, 11/28/08 [http://www.time.com/time/specials/2007/article/0,28804,1714683_1714625,00.html].

[121] Marie Glenn. "Maturing with the Millennials: Are Organisations Prepared for the Millennial Consumer?" *The Economist: Economist Intelligence Unit*, September 2008, 11/28/08 [http://viewswire.eiu.com/report_dl.asp?mode=fi&fi=493863234.PDF&rf=0].

[122] "Millennial Engagement," *What Do You Stand For?*, August 18, 2008, 11/28/08 [http://www.doyoustandforsomething.com/2008/08/millennial-enga.html].

online advertising. As discussed in a presentation by Digital Bridges, many companies are responding with Millennial-friendly strategies. For example, Nike has created NikeID.com, where customers can design their own sneakers using an online program.[123] This capitalizes nicely on the Millennial desire for customized customer experiences, just like the tailored educational experiences that prospective business school students are shopping around to find.

It is of course worth noting that the most important aspect of customization for which Millennial consumers thirst is the coalescence of the stated ideals of the company with their personal value system. In the 2006 Cone Millennial Cause Study, which presented the findings of an online survey conducted among a national sample of 1,800 Millennial respondents (ages 13-25), 74 percent of those who were surveyed responded that they are more likely to pay attention to a company when they see that it has a significant commitment to a cause. Some other fascinating data points on this:

- 83% will trust a company more if it
  is socially/environmentally responsible.

- 69% consider a company's social/environmental commitment
  when deciding where to shop.

- 89% are likely or very likely to switch from one brand to another
  (price and quality being equal) if the second brand is
  associated with a good cause.

- 66% will consider a company's social/environmental commitment
  when deciding whether to recommend its products and services.[124]

Ethos™ Water is an interesting example of a company that may be capitalizing well on this particular Millennial perspective. According to a March 2006 Business Week online article, "In roughly four years, Ethos™ Water...

---

[123] "The Millennial Market," presentation by Digital Bridges 2.0, 11/28/08
[http://www.digitalbridges20.net/files/Millennial%20Market%20PPT.pdf].

[124] "Cone 2006 Millennial Cause Study," *Cause Marketing Forum*,
October 24, 2006, 11/28/08
[http://www.causemarketingforum.com/page.asp?ID=473].

has grown from a local bottled water company selling its goods through yoga studios and health-food stores in Southern California, to a nationally recognized brand. Last year, the company was sold to Starbucks for $8 million, giving it a new distribution channel and substantially greater reach. That new market reach translated to more than just sales. It helps Ethos™ realize its underlying mission: to help children around the world get clean water."[125] The Ethos™ website describes its mission as follows: "[b]y purchasing Ethos™ Water, customers can join a growing community of individuals who are committed to make a difference. For each bottle of Ethos Water purchased, $0.05 will be donated towards Starbucks' goal to making $10 million in grant commitments toward humanitarian water programs by 2010."[126]

The *Business Week* article describes Ethos™ Water as "selling activism in a bottle."[127] Even as Scanlon questioned the company's founders, Jonathan Greenblatt and Peter Thum, regarding the concerns that had recently arisen over the issues in the bottled water industry, such as the lack of true need for bottled water in the American society of fully available potable (and healthy) drinking water, the existence of toxic chemicals in the bottles themselves, and the carbon footprint from the production of these bottles, Greenblatt and Thum articulated their appeal in the marketplace for conscientious consumers:

*Thum:*
"I don't think that we can answer for the entire bottled-water industry. What we're trying to do is make the American public aware of this problem [lack of access to clean water] – a problem that kills more people than AIDS. The bottled-water industry may not be perfect, but if you can take a sliver of the industry and turn it towards something positive, that's a good thing. The most important thing is to start a dialogue and to get people in the U.S. to

---

[125] Jessie Scanlon. "Buy Water, Help Children" *Business Week Online*, March 22, 2006, 12/10/08 [http://www.businessweek.com/print/investor/content/mar2006/pi20060322_252796.htm].

[126] Ethos Water website, [http://ethoswater.com/index.cfm?objectid=6407087F-F1F6-6035-B92627341D882A12].

[127] Jessie Scanlon. "Buy Water, Help Children" *Business Week Online*, March 22, 2006, 12/10/08 [http://www.businessweek.com/print/investor/content/mar2006/pi20060322_252796.htm].

start thinking about the world water crisis not just as something that affects people far away, but as a problem that we will face soon as well."

*Greenblatt:*

"When we launched the business, there were more than 700 brands. Now there are more than 800. With the entry of Coca-Cola and Pepsi into the market, scale certainly matters, so we might see some small brands disappear. But there's always the opportunity for niche brands that have a high value proposition."[128]

So for a generation that comprises such a strong consumer market and is so desirous of material goods, it is fascinating (and pretty important) to see that a company's message and mission plays so resoundingly in their purchasing decisions. This may be increasingly important if the economy continues with its current downturn. As Millennials work hard in the jobs that align with their personal value system, experience the professional success that they have always been told is theirs for the asking, and make the kind of money they believe is their due, they will want to spend that money on products and services about which they can feel okay. Millennials are the newest and maybe most enthusiastic conscientious consumers.

And they certainly apply this same brand of consumerism as they are looking to "purchase" their place of employment. You are again trying to recruit a new generation to your workforce who are making particularly informed decisions about where they are going to work. *So, if you want to attract and retain these employees: what do you do?*

- **Have a conscientious mission.**
  The message here...if you want to recruit a Millennial to come to work at your organization, be prepared to answer some tough questions about what your company stands for, and how prospective employees can find meaning in their work and feel good about the company's calling and the way in which it conducts its business.

*"I have found the generation entering the workforce now to be very enthusiastic, committed to social responsibility and sustainability efforts, eager to learn and contribute."*
Irene DeNigris
Director, Global University Recruitment Johnson & Johnson

---

[128] Ibid.

If a Millennial makes these values-driven decisions regarding the places where they will shop, the products that they will buy, and the companies that they will support with their well-earned money, we must recognize that these same values are applied to where they choose to work. If they won't buy a product from a company that reflects poor social and environmental commitments, then they are certainly going to think more than twice about working at an organization that doesn't align with their value system.

- **Consider tailoring the job to the individual.**

The message here...if you want to recruit a Millennial to come to work at your organization, be prepared to answer some tough questions about what your company stands for, and how prospective employees can find meaning in their work and feel good about the company's calling and the way in which it conducts its business.

To a generation raised on reaction to their needs and wants – at home, school, and society overall – customization from their workplace does not seem like an outlandish expectation. Be prepared that Millennial employees may want to have their jobs adapted to their specific professional interests and strengths. And this may not be such a terrible idea. If your organization can find the proverbial "right fit" for a job opening, then the job can be essentially tailored to the person in the position. If you are able to recruit and retain a team that collectively meets the needs to get the job the done, then you may be able to allow each member of the team to craft what element of the jobs fits in their purview. This is much easier said than done, however, and certainly the common business philosophy has generally been to NOT design the job around the person, but this may be another example of how times are changing. Certainly with increased teaming on projects and programs, a somewhat natural outcome is the parsing out of responsibilities based on skills, strengths, and interest.

- **Engage them.**

You need to be prepared to provide a voice to Millennial employees so that they feel fully connected to the mission of the organization; remember, throughout their lives, Millennials have always heard of the value of their input and the brilliance of their ideas.

*"Overall, the team environment is becoming more holistically embraced than the autocratic, corporate environments of the past. Society is awakening to the fact that everyone in the organization has a voice and experience that can contribute to the overall success of the business at hand."*
Mason Gates
President, Internships.com

A more democratic and consensus-oriented organizational structure holds tremendous appeal to Millennials, who often judge their choices for place of employment around environmental appeal. *What Millennial Workers Want: How to Attract and Retain Gen Y Employees* reports "[t]hose that are just starting their careers want to know that their contributions matter and their skills are improving. To close the revolving door, you may need to restructure the entry level positions, perhaps combining several functions to create a single, more challenging job, or developing a more defined path of advancement out of a routine role."[129]

Back in 2000, when they first published *Millennials Rising: The Next Great Generation*, Howe and Strauss were already suggesting that "Millennials are already the most achievement-oriented collegians in our nation's history, and by the time they leave the campus gates, they may be the most learned and capable graduates ever."[130] This is high praise and high pressure for a generation whose oldest representatives are in their mid 20's. But they seem to rise to the inherent challenges in many ways, and certainly their hopefulness and social-mindedness – even amidst these difficult economic times – bodes well for them as the rising generation in all areas: government, business, education, religion, etc. We need "Generation Optimistic" to help to lead the charge.

---

[129] Robert Half International and YAHOO! Hot Jobs, "What Millennial Workers Want: How to Attract and Retain Gen Y Employees," (California, 2007) 15.

[130] Neil Howe and William Strauss, *Millennials Rising: The Next Great Generation,* (New York: Vintage Books, 2000).

## CHAPTER SIX: SUMMARY

- Millennials are an extremely politically active generation, with much of their activity taking place online via social media; this is something upon which Barrack Obama very successfully capitalized during the 2008 presidential election.

- Research indicates that Millennials think that political engagement is an effective way of solving important issues facing the country and disagree with the notion often held by previous generations that if the federal government runs something, it is necessarily inefficient and wasteful.

- Utilization of an inclusionary and consensus-oriented approach has great appeal to the Millennials, a generation that is quite used to teaming and groupwork.

- One major question that remains, as the economy continues with its current downturn is, will Millennials, who have really mostly seen overall societal prosperity during their collective upbringing, find their perspective on their world shaken by new economic developments? Past experience and newer data suggests that it may be that they see opportunity for betterment coming from all of this, and that they see themselves at the heart of this change, as Millennials are typified by their optimism and a common desire to make the world a better place.

- Companies will benefit from overhauling their employee recruitment materials to bring attention to their community service and environmental initiatives, in their efforts to attract the interest of prospective Millennial employees.

- Companies can also capitalize on the Millennial desire for customized customer experiences, including by paying attention to Millennials' focus on social and environmental responsibility as conscientious consumers.

- As organizations work to attract and retain Millennial employees, it will be important to maintain and promote a conscientious mission, consider tailoring jobs to the individual, and provide a voice to Millennial employees, so that they feel fully connected to the mission of the organization.

# CLOSING

## Millennials - The Intriguing Generation? Resisted.

I continue to find Millennials to be one of the more fascinating groups I've encountered, and the study of them to be among the most fascinating topics. They have a strong community culture, a vibrant group and individual personality, and are poised to make their impact on the world, including the work world. In fact, as I maintain throughout this book, they already are making this impact. They have led the way in technology, forcing organizations to amp up their services and equipment, while teaching those of us who are older how to succeed in a digital world. They push us to reconsider how we offer feedback to employees – not just how often, but in what ways. They have encouraged the development of more robust programs and services designed to support employees through difficult personal and professional circumstances. They promote optimistic views of the world and the need for companies to engage in missions and activities that are socially responsible and of benefit to more than just the shareholders.

So who are the Millennials? Are they a "Hovered Generation," whose parents loom large and pervade all aspects of their lives, including being engaged in all of their professional experiences and decisions? Are they "Generation RX," a group so overstressed and overwhelmed that their workplace functioning is directly impacted? Are they "Generation 2.0," so tech-oriented and tech-savvy that they are both leaders of and detractors to workplace functioning? Are they the "Programmed Generation," an assemblage so accustomed to engaging in activities in groups that are led by authorities that they are now great team-players—but they may be paralyzed when having to accomplish anything on their own? Are they a "Celebrated Generation," cultivated to have a strong sense of self that borders on hubris, and to expect near-constant feedback – hopefully in the form of praise – so that anything less makes for an unacceptable professional situation? Are they "Generation Optimistic," ready to lead the world to a better place and filled with an ideology of social responsibility? I think they are all of these things and more. They have much to offer to our workplaces, and along with that much of which to be mindful. They are shaping the nature of the workplace. They are the future and the future has arrived.

Throughout this book, I provide suggestions for ways that companies can work with their Millennial employees, integrating them into the overall organizational culture, and just as important, some ways in which companies can work within their own organization, integrating it into the overall Millennial culture. I am fully aware of the fact that Millennials have some learning and growing to do, and certainly need to build their professional maturity and skill sets to succeed in the work environment, but our work atmospheres need to evolve as well. It is not just an issue of Millennials being a new major force in the professional world, and we have to adjust whether we want to or not...we should want to! Millennials bring a great deal of hope, determination, skills, and ideas from which organizations can benefit significantly if we allow ourselves to shed the antiquated notion that only the more experienced colleagues have value to contribute to the larger workplace issues and conversations. We are not using these young employees well if we only engage them in less important roles or conversations. We are losing potential growth opportunities with such missteps. So, here are some of the major takeaways that come up in these chapters (in far more detail) as potential responses to the issues and characteristics I've discussed:

- **We need to educate all members of the workplace on generational differences.**
Clearly there are many generation gaps between Millennials and those who came before them, and these are causing a lot of workplace disconnect. Understanding – by all parties – of each other is an essential ingredient in overcoming these challenges.

- **Feedback is SO important.**
And it is not just that giving feedback is important; that isn't new. But just how important is more novel, as is the focus on how it is provided: more of it, more frequently, and a more carefully considered delivery.

- **Involve parents.**

They play a huge role in the lives of their adult children, and engaging them to some degree will serve you well. Consider seminars, newsletters, and other resources to respond to their questions and concerns. Just keep in mind that boundaries are very important as well!

- **Provide developmental opportunities.**

Millennials, arguably more so than previous generations of young people, have lots of room to grow, and the work atmosphere is poised to support this maturing. Through developmental supervision, mentoring and coaching, and professional development programs, this can be advanced.

- **Educate on workplace behavior expectations.**

When we talk about crucial areas for growth, workplace protocol is a primary area that needs edification in no sphere more than that of appropriate technology usage.

- **Recognize what Millennials have to offer.**

Look to the areas that are of great strength for Millennials, and "give them voice." Not only will this provide suitable and welcomed validation, but it is of great benefit to the organization, especially around technology, efficiencies, and teaming. Reverse-mentorship programs can be are a great element of this!

- **Enhance your existing technologies.**

You will need to do this to recruit and retain the candidates you are seeking, and it will certainly help with any virtual teaming or workplace-flexible staffing options that you hope to employ.

- **Capitalize on your organization's conscientious mission.**

If you don't have one, it may be time to consider this. As concepts like social responsibility and sustainability continue coming to the fore – not just for Millennials, but certainly quite forcefully for them – this too is a key element in attracting and retaining this new generation. And this is not just for them as employees but also as potential consumers of your products and services. This is key to their engagement.

- **Think about customizing jobs.**

Millennials are used to things being tailored to them, and they will seek out environments that seem to offer this. Most of the places that I have worked have talked about how "you don't form the job around the person," yet I find that it happens quite a bit...and it could be a good thing. This is more of a new trend, but maybe it's time has come.

To be sure, Millennials are leading us towards a new place, and there is much room and opportunity for progress. I discuss throughout this book the challenges of considering Millennials' future and roles in our organizations when so many workplaces find themselves constantly shifting and changing amidst our current economic uncertainties. Research on this has only just begun, and it suggests that further investigation and analysis of this issue is called for. Regardless of the changing picture of the economy and its impact on workplace dynamics, we are charged.

# RECOMMENDED READINGS

**Millennials - Extra, Extra, Read All About Them.**

I have done a lot of reading about Millennials over the years, and have found several resources that I recommend to any interested reader. There is a lot of stuff out there about this generation; as I mentioned in the introduction, I can't seem to walk into a bookstore without buying at least one new book on the topic. On top of that, I am always tearing articles out of newspapers or magazines that I find pertinent to the topic in one way or another, and of course I also print things off the web at least once a week – as a creature of technology myself, despite my Luddite claims! If you find that this book has only piqued your interest in this most fascinating generation and their unique characteristics, then you may find these of interest as well.

- ***Millennials Rising: The Next Great Generation***
  **by William Strauss and Neil Howe. Vintage Books (2000).**
  At least for me, this is the book that began it all. Strauss and Howe have been on the forefront of generation research overall, and they are the ones who coined the term "Millennial." Obviously, there have been many other researchers who write extensively about this generation, and use some of the other terminology to refer to them – like Echo Boomers or Boomlets, Generation Y, or Generation NeXt – but Strauss and Howe did it first and did it pretty well. While I have always had concerns about the narrow pool from which their research draws, and the fact that those who have not achieved middle class or higher may not be effectively represented in their data, they nonetheless provide an interesting lens through which to look at the psychography of the generation. These guys discuss Millennials by ascribing them seven core traits, which I have found to be an extremely helpful way to understand and frame this psychography. It may sometimes seem like generalizations, but the characteristics usually resonate deeply with Millennials and those who parent, teach, and work with them.

If you want something that is a bit more concise, their follow-up *Millennials Go to College* (2003) provides a nice synopsis with an updated slant. Bear in mind that the focus of this one is Millennials' potential impact on and experience of the college environs.

- *College of the Overwhelmed:*
  *The Campus Mental Health Crisis and What To Do About It*
  **by Dr. Richard Kadison. Jossey-Bass (2004).**

This book was written as a resource not simply for college administrators, but also for parents. Beyond that, however, it serves as a tremendous source of relevant data and discusses many of the concerning trends in mental health in a coherent and effective way. Dr. Kadison provides excellent information and analysis about emotional and psychological concerns for today's late adolescents and young adults (those of the Millennial Generation), and while it may be framed around their presence on our college campuses, there is bearing for those who work with and supervise Millennials in the professional environment. If you have experienced any kind of rise in personal issues impacting the work life of any of your young employees, this book may be surprisingly relevant and useful.

- *A Nation of Wimps: The High Cost of Invasive Parenting*
  **by Hara Estroff Marano. Broadway Books (2008).**

I am always concerned with the fact that the issues that seem to plague the prototypical Millennials do not have to do with getting basic needs met, but in fact often have to do with being over-resourced. Marano's discussion of the way parental intervention and – dare I say it? – coddling of children has led to what some call an epidemic of young people unable to deal with the normal hurdles of life. Understanding the societal and psychological root of the emotional "handicaps" of Millennials may help you to better understand their issues and limitations in the work environment. At the very least, this book provides a really fascinating, though quite concerning, look at how the child-rearing trends and philosophies of the last couple of decades have had significant unintended consequences.

- *Too Much of a Good Thing: Raising Children of Character*
  *in an Indulgent Age*
  **by Dan Kindlon, Ph.D. Hyperion Books (2001).**

Like Marano's book, this too discusses the challenges that can come with affluence, or at least near affluence, though part of what I like about Kindlon's book is that is isn't necessarily as focused on those of greater means but really the age in which we all live. This book is geared to parents as a resource for child-rearing, but I think that Kindlon's research is sound and well-discussed, and it has been a useful tool for me in my work. His somewhat "cutesy" approach is to frame the issues around "the seven deadly sins" (pride, wrath, envy, etc.), but it actually comes off pretty well.

- ***The Price of Privilege: How Parental Pressure and Material Advantage Are Creating a Generation of Disconnected and Unhappy Kids***
  **by Madeline Levine, Ph.D. HarperCollins Publishers (2006).**
  In a starker contrast to *Too Much of a Good Thing*, Levine really maintains a direct focus on children from quite financially advantaged situations. She is a clinical psychologist who works with children and adolescents in a very affluent community, and this has informed this work by design. She explores the environmental influences and parental practices that most of the young people in her practice face, and concludes that they are often of detriment to healthy development. Again, this is really slanted work, but when we talk about the most "prototypical Millennials," this is some useful and stimulating information.

- **"The Echo Boomers,"** *60 Minutes*, **September 4, 2005.**
  This is a pretty interesting report, and does a nice job of painting a picture about Millennials through interviews with Millennials among the experts; thus we get a discussion of some of the issues in Millennials' own words,. The segment was only about 15 minutes or so long, but it is thoroughly engaging and informative. I think it can still be purchased from 60 Minutes' website for about ten bucks, and I believe it is worth it.

- **"The Organization Kid" by David Brooks.** <u>The Atlantic</u>, **April 2001.**
  Like the *60 Minutes* piece, Brooks' 2001 article for *The Atlantic* is a noteworthy summation of what the Millennial Generation is all about. The focus is on their hyper-programming, but it frames many of the other unintended consequences around that. Brooks provides a window into who they are and how their upbringing has informed their outlook. The earliest Millennials had really just hit college when this came out, but I don't think the fact that it is a bit dated at this point makes it lose meaning or relevance to who these Millennials are now.

- *Unequal Childhoods: Class, Race, and Family Life*
  **by Annette Lareau. University of California Press (2003).**

  The focus of this book is not simply on Millennials, but it is actually an ethnographic study that examines the difference that social class makes in the lives of children. As someone who is very interested in issues of socio-economics, particularly with regard to access to educational and other opportunity, Lareau's work is really interesting. It also helps to fill in a bit of the gaps that I find in direct research on Millennials themselves – namely whether the issues are the same for all regardless of demographics like race and social class.

- *Born Digital: Understanding the First Generation of Digital Natives*
  **by John Palfrey and Urs Gasser. Basic Books (2008).**

  I have long-maintained that technology has had a more significant influence on Millennials' psychography than anything else, except their parents of course, and reading this book has confirmed that for me. Palfrey and Gasser call this generation "digital natives" and explain the vast differences between them and those who precede them, who they refer to as "digital immigrants." They have some interesting ideas about how these young people have been shaped by the ubiquitous presence of technology in their lives, and they also contemplate how they – and their tech-orientation – will transform the future of our economy, politics, culture, and family life.

 Rachel I. Reiser is the founder and principle of Generationally Speaking; Generationally Speaking provides consultation to companies and other organizations in helping them to consider their work in the age of the Millennial Generation. Rachel is also currently Associate Dean for Academic Services at Babson College in Wellesley, MA.

In a career spanning over 15 years in higher education, Rachel has held positions at several schools working directly with college students, providing her with the opportunity to experience first-hand the changing characteristics of today's late adolescent. This, coupled with her own observations, has fostered her professional interest in generational studies. Rachel has researched, written, and presented extensively on the demographics and psychographics of the Millennial generation.

Rachel is an active member of several professional organizations, and is the 2006 recipient of the Massachusetts Association for Women in Education Award for Professional Excellence.

Rachel can be reached at rreiser@genspeaks.com.

# NOTES

# NOTES

# NOTES

# NOTES

# NOTES

# NOTES

# NOTES

# NOTES

# NOTES